BEYON_

A JOURNEY TO MINDFUL

PUBLIC SPEAKING

A QUEST TO TOUCH THE

HEARTS, MINDS

& SOULS OF BILLIONS

BY ROHIT BASSI

CONTENTS

FOREWARD

Working with NASA breaking the boundaries of spirituality and technology, I learned that communication is how we all connect as humans and how we move humanity forward together.

Communication is key to getting things done, building connections, and moving the world forward. In my 25-year journey of helping organisations grow, I've seen first-hand that success often comes down to how well we communicate. If messages aren't clear at the basic level, nothing else works as it should. And this is just as true the other way around. I've had the chance to work with big names like NASA, Kearney, Google, Microsoft, and many Fortune 500 companies. In these places, making sure communication works well is a big challenge. What really matters is being able to create a clear message and make sure it's heard.

This is where Rohit has played a huge role in my career. He's been a mentor and a leader, showing me how to get my points across clearly and effectively, whether I'm speaking to a large audience or discussing strategy in a boardroom.

But Rohit taught me that communicating well is about more than just getting messages across; it's also about understanding and empathy. Being able to see things from someone else's perspective can help you connect with anyone, no matter how different your backgrounds or languages might be. This lesson has been a game-changer for me, making me a much better communicator.

When I speak to groups of people, I think a lot about why they decided to listen to me in the first place. Every time I give a talk, I know people are there for their own reasons—maybe they want to be inspired, learn something new, check their own ideas, or see things from a different angle. Whatever their reasons, they're looking for some kind of change. As a speaker, it's my job to help make that change happen, even if I only have 10 minutes with them.

Rohit is like a wizard when it comes to communication. He knows how to blend kindness, a strong presence, and the skill to craft and share powerful messages. His guidance has been crucial for me, not alone in my career, but in how I connect with people in all areas of my life.

Nader Sabry is a strategist, innovator, and entrepreneur in NASA space tech, government, *and health/wellness. Has raised $20m directly /+$100m indirectly for start-ups and is a bestselling author of "Ready Set growth Hack: A beginners guide to growth hacking success" which is a growth blueprint for organisations to achieve 10x growth.*

ACKNOWLEDGEMENT

This book, shaped by both nurturing support and life's rigorous trials, stands as a testament to compassion, resilience, and antifragility. I am deeply grateful to my family, friends, and mentors, whose unwavering support has been as vital as rain to a seedling.

The challenges I've faced along the way have not only tested me but have deepened the roots of this work, infusing it with a unique strength and depth. This book is more than just a collection of pages; it is a refuge for thought and a beacon of shared experience, offering comfort and insight to anyone who opens its pages.

Created with originality at its heart, this work draws from a diverse array of inspirations. Any similarities to existing works are purely coincidental, as my goal has always been to offer something both unique and valuable.

To ensure the quality of this book, I have utilized AI technology and enlisted the expertise of professional editors and proof-readers.

My aim is to inspire and contribute my voice to a wider conversation, without any intent of copying someone else's work. This book reflects my personal journey, marked by experiences, extensive reading, and the invaluable lessons learned from my mistakes. It is crafted with the intention of sharing my insights and understandings in a way that is both meaningful and beneficial to you, the beloved reader.

One Billion Voices: The Quest for Mindful Communication

Dear Reader,

Before we embark on this journey together, I want to share with you a deeply personal dream—a vision that fuels every word written here.

My Dream: Be A Part of One Billion Voices

Before I leave this world, I am driven by a powerful dream. It is not a goal but a heartfelt aspiration: to share the knowledge, science, and art of public speaking with 1 billion people. This dream transcends teaching methods, techniques, or sharing strategies. It's about inspiring a global shift in how we communicate.

Why This Matters: The World We Live In

In our world of leaders, decision-makers, and influencers, we often witness communication driven by selfishness, manipulation, and a lack of genuine connection. This unhealthy approach creates relationships, businesses, communities, and environments that are toxic and hostile. Such an unhealthy approach to communication impacts our existence.

The Seed of Mindful Communication

My aim is simple: to plant and nurture the seed of mindful communication. This isn't just about speaking well; it's about speaking with wholesome intention, care, and compassion. You may say I am a dreamer, as I envision a world where our words are not weapons but bridges, connecting us in ways that are respectful, empathetic, and uplifting.

Envisioning a Joyful, Loving World

Through mindful communication, we can create a world that is truly joyful, loving, and caring. It's about moving away from manipulative tactics and embracing an approach where our words, feelings, and actions are filled with courage, clarity, conviction, and compassion.

The Power of Public Speaking

Public speaking is a potent tool in this endeavour. Let us move away from the myth and lies of "Sticks and stones may break my bones, but words will never hurt me."

This phrase, while often used to teach resilience against verbal insults, overlooks the significant impact that words can have.

It's not about addressing an audience; it's about engaging hearts and minds and encouraging conversations beyond mere words.

Through the art and science of public speaking, we can empower individuals to express themselves authentically and mindfully.

Your Role in This Journey

As you turn these pages, you're doing more than just learning to be a great speaker. You're becoming a part of a larger movement towards mindful communication. Each chapter, each concept, and each exercise are a step towards a world were communication fosters kindness.

Together, we can

Help me in this mission. Join me in encouraging, engaging, and empowering not ourselves alone but a billion minds towards the path of mindful communication. Let's transform to become wholesome in the way we speak, listen, and connect.

Let's Begin

As we delve into the chapters of this book, I invite you to embark on this journey, not as a reader but as an ally in this vision.

Together, let's explore how the timeless wisdom of public speaking can be a catalyst for a world more connected, more understanding, and profoundly more compassionate.

With trust and determination,

Rohit Bassi
www.rohitbassi.com

Defining Key Terms

Before we embark on our journey, it's essential to ensure we're on the same page. We'll begin by clarifying the meanings of key words and terms that form the foundation of our discussions.

These definitions are shared at the outset to provide a common understanding of the concepts we'll encounter along the way. Join us as we dive into the essence of authentic communication and its impact on our relationships and personal growth.

Authenticity: Being genuine in every word and engaging listeners. Authenticity lays the foundation for strong relationships in communication. It's about staying true to oneself, and the message fosters honesty and integrity in every interaction. It builds trust and credibility with the audience, breaking down pretences and fostering a genuine connection. Authenticity is the soul of impactful communication, revealing the human behind the words and turning a speech into a heartfelt conversation.

Public speaking: Sharing ideas to truly connect with listeners. It engages audiences, fostering relationships and genuine rapport. Public speaking involves speaking from the heart with the touch of intelligence. Ensuring sincerity in every word and creating an environment where both the speaker and the listener can grow. It encourages openness and vulnerability, enhances connection, and becomes a bridge between individuals. It's not about conveying information but about building a community of understanding that is transformative when done with intention and mindfulness.

Presentation: Conveying messages and engaging intelligence, senses and emotions. It builds relationships through structured, visual storytelling, combining personal truth with audience awareness. A presentation is more than data; it's a narrative that resonates, engaging more than the mind but also the heart of the audience. It creates a shared space for exploration and understanding, inviting participation and empowering both the presenter and the audience with new perspectives. It's a journey of collective discovery and connection.

Communication: This is honest exchange that engages and connects. Healthy communication builds lasting relationships, serving as the cornerstone of human interaction and understanding. Communication goes beyond words; it's about sharing experiences and emotions that involve listening as much as speaking to create a balanced dialogue. It builds bridges across differences, fostering inclusivity, transparency, and trust, ultimately transforming individuals and communities. It's a powerful tool for personal, career, business, and societal growth.

Mindfulness: Presence enhances connection and engagement, nurturing understanding and deepening relationships in communication. It's about being fully there, with and for your audience. Encourages active listening and responding with empathy and care. Mindfulness transforms communication into a reflective practice, fostering a space of mutual respect and openness. It breaks down barriers, revealing shared humanity and about being in the moment with complete attention and sincerity, and cultivates a communication style that's both grounded and profound.

Wholesome: Communication characterised by purity, kindness, and heartfelt sincerity. It's like a ray of sunshine on a clear day, radiating positivity and goodwill. Wholesome communication seeks to create a nurturing atmosphere where relationships can thrive and grow. It's the embodiment of genuine care and consideration in every word and gesture, fostering deep connections.

Mindflow: Being in flow creates genuine engagement. Mindflow forges deeper connections, enhancing speaker-audience relationships. It's the harmony of being and expressing in unison. Allows ideas to be shared fluidly, without barriers. Mindflow, like a river, naturally navigates the landscape of interaction, encouraging creative spontaneity and connection. It breaks down the walls of formal communication, fostering intimacy and sync with oneself and the audience, enabling a communication style that's effective and effortless. This is not mindset which makes you set in your ways.

Non-Verbal Communication: Gestures and expressions engage and build trust, strengthening relationships beyond words. Non-verbal's convey emotions and intentions, enhancing the impact of verbal communication, reflecting the speaker's true feelings, and breaking down barriers when words are insufficient. A smile, a gesture, a look—all speak volumes, crucial in building empathy and understanding without uttering a word—the unspoken poetry of interaction.

Engagement: Being interactive enriches the communication experience thus fosters great relationships. It's about creating a two-way street in conversation that encourages active participation and genuine interest, builds a dynamic environment where ideas flourish, and transforms passive listening into active collaboration. Engagement is the heartbeat of effective communication, fostering community and shared purpose in dialogue.

Adaptability: Adaptability engages diverse audiences, nurturing relationships across contexts by audience where they are and tailoring messages to resonate with different perspectives. It allows for fluid and responsive communication, embracing diversity as an opportunity for richer interaction. Adaptability is the key to relevance and connection. It's about being open to change and growth. Creates a communication style that's both versatile and impactful.

Resilience: By staying true and engaged through challenges, resilient communicators build enduring relationships, bounce back with grace and learning, and maintain a positive and constructive approach in adversity. It strengthens the speaker's bond with the audience through shared struggles, encouraging growth and continuous improvement, and transforming obstacles into opportunities for connection with enduring toughness and a soft heart.

Antifragility: Gaining strength from adversity in communication. Improving and growing through challenges, embracing disruption as an opportunity for growth, and thriving under pressure, not merely surviving, turns every challenge into a chance to enhance skills, building a dynamic and evolving communication style, embracing uncertainty, and creating a resilient, adaptive, and powerful communication presence.

In a world often filled with noise, the power of mindful communication stands out as a beacon of authenticity and empathy. It's a reminder of the power of kindness and the value of human connection. When we engage in mindful communication, we uplift ourselves and those around us, creating a ripple effect of positivity and harmony.

Chapter 1: The 1st Universal Truth – Understanding the Core of Communication

Embracing the Essence

Welcome to our journey together. Imagine we're sitting in a comfortable, quiet space, perhaps with a beverage of your choice in hand, ready to delve into a conversation that would change the way you approach communication. The first universal truth we're going to explore is a practical foundation for effective communication. Let's unwrap this together, shall we?

The Truth of Connection

At its heart, communication is about connection. When you speak, it's more than words that are exchanged; it's emotions, ideas, and energies. Think about it: for every great speech you've ever heard, wasn't it the speaker's ability to connect with you that made it memorable?

The Reality of Perception

Now, consider this: your audience's perception is their reality. What you say might be factual and informative, but how you say it and how you make them feel—that's what sticks. Have you ever noticed how the same message can be interpreted differently by different people? That's the power of perception at play.

The Art of Listening

Effective communication is a two-way street. You must integrate the skill of mindful speaking with the grace of listening. More than waiting to say your part, it's about really knowing and caring for your listener. Can you recall a time when you felt genuinely heard? How did that make you feel about the speaker?

The Power of Authenticity

Authenticity is your greatest ally. In a world filled with scripted talks and rehearsed speeches, authenticity stands out. Being authentic to both your message and yourself is key. When was the last time you spoke from your heart, unguarded and sincere?

Practical Exercise: Mirror of Communication

Now, let's engage in a simple but effective exercise. For one minute, stand in front of a mirror and discuss something that truly interests you. Watch yourself. Notice your facial expressions, your gestures, and the tone of your voice. Are you just speaking, or are you also conveying? Are you connecting with the person in the mirror?

Reflecting On the Truth

As we conclude this chapter, reflect on how you've communicated in the past. It's not really about the information you've shared, but the connections you've made. The essence of communication is building a shared understanding. We're learning more than good speaking; we're learning to connect deeply and genuinely. Take this idea with you and let it inform how you speak and engage with others.

NOTES

_____

_____

_____

_____

_____

_____

_____

_____

_____

_____

_____

_____

_____

_____

_____

_____

_____

_____

_____

_____

_____

_____

_____

_____

_____

_____

_____

_____

_____

_____

_____

_____

_____

_____

_____

_____

_____

_____

_____

_____

_____

_____

Chapter 2: The 2nd Universal Truth – Embracing Change and Adaptability in Public Speaking

Welcome to Our Continuing Conversation

As we delve into the second chapter of our journey, imagine we're resuming our dialogue in that cosy, warm and inviting setting. Picture yourself growing more comfortable and engaged, as we explore another deep aspect of communication.

The Nature of Change

The second universal truth revolves around the inevitability of change and the power of adaptability. In the realm of public speaking, this truth plays a pivotal role. Let's unpack this together.

Change: The Only Constant

In every aspect of life, change is a constant. As a public speaker, you'll encounter diverse audiences, varying environments, and evolving topics. How you adapt to these changes determines not merely the effectiveness of your communication but also your growth as a speaker.

Adaptability: Your Secret Weapon

Think of adaptability as your secret weapon. It's about being flexible and versatile in your approach. Adjusting your style to suit the audience, the setting, and the context. Remember a time when you had to unexpectedly change your approach during a conversation or presentation. How did it feel? More importantly, how did you handle it?

The Dance of Speaking

Public speaking is like a dance. You lead, but you also follow. You plan, but you also improvise. Every audience interaction is an opportunity to adjust your rhythm, to sync with their energy and expectations. How do you feel when a speaker seems attuned to their audience's reactions and adjusts accordingly?

Embracing Flexibility in Your Message

Your message is important, but its delivery needs to be flexible. Think of your core message as a tree – strong and steady – but your delivery like its branches, swaying and adapting to the winds of your audience's moods and reactions.

Practical Exercise: The Adaptability Scenario

Let's engage in a practical exercise. Imagine you're in a conversation and suddenly you notice your listener's attention waning. Pause for a moment in your scenario. How would you pivot? Maybe you'd inject a story, change your tone, or invite interaction. Practice this pivot. How does the shift in approach feel?

Reflecting On the Truth

As we conclude this chapter, reflect on the nature of change and your response to it. Embracing change and cultivating adaptability is more than altering your words, but about tuning into the dynamic energy of your listeners. It's about being aware, in the moment, ready to shift your approach for maximum engagement and impact.

NOTES

_____

_____

_____

_____

_____

_____

_____

_____

_____

_____

_____

_____

_____

_____

_____

_____

_____

_____

_____

_____

_____

_____

_____

_____

_____

_____

_____

_____

_____

_____

_____

_____

_____

_____

_____

_____

_____

_____

Chapter 3: The 3rd Universal Truth – Navigating and Overcoming Speaking Challenges

Resuming Our Intimate Dialogue

As we embark on this next chapter, imagine us deepening our conversation, like two old friends uncovering life's mysteries. Here, in our shared space of learning and growth, we're about to explore a truth that's vital to your journey as a speaker.

Understanding the 3rd Universal Truth

The third universal truth is about recognising and overcoming the inherent challenges in communication. It's about facing what often goes unspoken: the fears, the anxieties, and the uncertainties that come with public speaking.

The Inevitability of Challenges

Speaking challenges are inevitable. Whether it's fear of judgment, struggling to articulate thoughts clearly, or managing audience reactions, every speaker faces these hurdles. Think back to a moment when you faced a speaking challenge. How did it make you feel? More importantly, how did you respond?

Transforming Challenges into Opportunities

Every challenge in speaking is an opportunity for growth. It's passing through your fears; recognizing them, learning from them, and using them as stepping-stones. How can your past challenges be re-framed as opportunities?

Embracing Vulnerability

Being vulnerable holds immense power in communication. It's about sharing your personal challenges and fears, not related to speaking or preparation, but those deeper, human experiences that everyone can relate to. This kind of openness fosters a deeper connection with your audience.

Reflect on times you've heard a speaker share their vulnerabilities. How did it affect your perception of them? This approach often leads to a more profound, authentic engagement, making the speaker more relatable and their message more impactful."

Role of Preparation, Preparation & Preparation
Preparation is your friend in overcoming speaking challenges. It's about knowing your material well enough that you can adapt it on the fly. How do you currently prepare for speeches? Could there be room for improvement?

Practical Exercise: The Challenge Reversal

Let's engage in a practical exercise. Think of a specific speaking challenge you've faced. Now, write it down. Next to it, write down a positive outcome or learning experience that came from it. For example, if your challenge was 'fear of forgetting my speech,' the positive outcome could be 'learning to speak more naturally without relying entirely on my notes.'

Reflecting On the Truth

As we conclude this chapter, take a moment to reflect on the challenges you've faced in speaking. How can the acknowledgment and understanding of these challenges empower you? How can they transform your approach to public speaking and communication?

NOTES

_____

_____

_____

_____

_____

_____

_____

_____

_____

_____

_____

_____

_____

_____

_____

_____

_____

_____

_____

_____

_____

_____

_____

_____

_____

_____

_____

_____

_____

_____

_____

_____

_____

_____

_____

_____

_____

_____

_____

_____

_____

Chapter 4: The 1st Noble Truth – Understanding Your Audience through Connection

Deepening Our Conversation

As we turn the page to a new chapter in our journey, imagine us sitting together once more, delving into the nuances of communication. This time, we explore a vital aspect of public speaking: understanding your audience through the lens of the first noble truth.

Unveiling the First Noble Truth

The first noble truth, in the context of public speaking, revolves around the inherent challenges of truly knowing your audience. It's about recognising that every audience comes with its own set of needs, perceptions, and expectations.

The Challenge of Audience Connection

Connecting with an audience can be more complex than it seems. Each individual in your audience carries their own unique background, beliefs, and biases. Have you ever noticed how a single message can resonate differently with different people?

The Art of Audience Analysis

Understanding and knowing your audience begins with keen observation and empathy. It's about putting you in their shoes and asking yourself: What are their concerns? What do they value? How can your message align with their worldview?

Listening Beyond Words

Listening is a powerful tool for understanding your audience. It's not about hearing their questions or comments but about picking up on non-verbal cues—the nods, the smiles, the puzzled expressions. Can you recall a time when you adjusted your conversation based on these subtle signals?

Practical Exercise: The Empathy Map

Let's engage in a practical exercise: create an empathy map. On a blank sheet of paper, divide it into four sections: thinking, feeling, seeing, and hearing. Imagine a member or persona of your audience and fill in these sections from their perspective related to your topic. This exercise can provide profound insights into your audience's mindflow.

Reflecting On the Truth

As we conclude this chapter, reflect on the diversity and complexity of your audience. Embracing this first noble truth is about acknowledging and understanding these complexities and using this understanding to forge a deeper, more meaningful connection.

NOTES

_____

_____

_____

_____

_____

_____

_____

_____

_____

_____

_____

_____

_____

_____

_____

_____

_____

_____

_____

_____

_____

_____

_____

_____

_____

_____

_____

_____

_____

_____

_____

_____

_____

_____

_____

_____

_____

_____

Chapter 5: The 2nd Noble Truth – Harnessing Persuasion through Understanding

Engaging in Our Continued Dialogue

As we progress in our journey together, let's sit back once again, envisioning a space of mutual exploration and growth. In this chapter, we delve into the second noble truth and its critical role in developing persuasive speaking skills.

Exploring the Second Noble Truth

The second noble truth in the context of public speaking is about recognising and addressing the root causes of disengagement or resistance in your audience. It's about understanding why certain messages resonate while others fall flat.

The Essence of Persuasion

Persuasion isn't just about convincing others; it's about understanding their needs, fears, and desires. Have you ever shifted someone's mind, not by overwhelming them with facts but by aligning your message with their core values?

The Role of Empathy in Persuasion

At the heart of persuasive speaking lies empathy. To persuade effectively, you need to step into your audience's shoes. What are their challenges? What keeps them up at night? How does your message provide a solution or relief?

The Power of Relevant Storytelling

Storytelling is a persuasive speaker's most potent tool. A well-told story can bridge gaps, build understanding, and create a shared experience. Think about a story that once captivated you—what elements made it impactful?

Practical Exercise: Persuasive Narrative

Let's engage in a practical exercise: craft a short, persuasive narrative based on your topic. Focus on creating a story that connects with your audience's values and experiences. How does your story address their concerns or aspirations? Give this a go and notice how it changes the impact of your message.

Reflecting On the Truth

As we wrap up this chapter, ponder the power of understanding the underlying reasons behind your audience's perspectives. This second noble truth is about using this insight to craft messages that's more than informing but also resonate and persuade.

NOTES

_____

_____

_____

_____

_____

_____

_____

_____

_____

_____

_____

_____

_____

_____

_____

_____

_____

_____

_____

_____

_____

_____

_____

_____

_____

_____

_____

_____

_____

_____

_____

_____

_____

_____

_____

_____

_____

_____

_____

_____

_____

Chapter 6: The 3rd Noble Truth – Overcoming Anxiety through Acceptance

Continuing our Heartfelt Conversation

As we gather once more in our shared space of learning, imagine us delving deeper into the essence of mindful communication. In this chapter, we'll explore the third noble truth and how embracing it can be a key to passing through public speaking anxiety.

Unveiling the Third Noble Truth

The third noble truth in public speaking is about acknowledging and accepting the inevitable anxieties and fears that accompany the act of speaking in front of others. It's a universal experience, but how we deal with this anxiety can transform our approach to speaking.

The Reality of Speaking Anxiety

Anxiety in public speaking is as natural as the nervousness one feels before any significant event. It's an acknowledgment of the importance of what you're about to do. Have you ever felt those butterflies before a talk? That's not really fear; it's also a sign of your commitment to delivering something valuable.

Embracing Anxiety, Not Resisting

The key is not to resist this anxiety but to embrace it. Resistance often amplifies fear, while acceptance brings clarity and calm. When was the last time you acknowledged your speaking anxiety and allowed yourself to feel it, without judgment or criticism?

The Role of Mindfulness

Mindfulness plays a crucial role here. It's about being present in the moment and acknowledging your feelings without being overwhelmed by them. Mindfulness practice can help you observe your anxiety, understand it, and gradually reduce its power over you.

Practical Exercise: Anxiety Acknowledgment

For our practical exercise, let's look at the anxiety acknowledgement. Sit quietly and think about an upcoming speaking engagement. Notice any feelings of anxiety that arise. Instead of pushing them away, acknowledge them. Say to yourself, "It's okay to feel anxious." Observe how this simple acknowledgment can ease your tension.

Reflecting On the Truth

As we conclude this chapter, reflect on how embracing your speaking anxiety, rather than fighting it, can be a transformative experience. This third noble truth teaches us that the path to passing through anxiety is about acceptance and mindfulness, not avoidance.

NOTES

_____

_____

_____

_____

_____

_____

_____

_____

_____

_____

_____

_____

_____

_____

_____

_____

_____

_____

_____

_____

_____

_____

_____

_____

_____

_____

_____

_____

_____

_____

_____

_____

_____

_____

_____

_____

_____

_____

_____

_____

_____

_____

Chapter 7: The 4th Noble Truth – Crafting Impactful Messages with Purpose

Engaging in a Deeper Exchange

As we continue our enriching dialogue, let's delve into the essence of the fourth noble truth and its profound implications for public speaking. This chapter invites us to discover how implementing this truth can guide us in crafting messages that resonate deeply and lastingly.

Understanding the 4th Noble Truth

The fourth noble truth in the realm of public speaking is about the path to crafting messages that are more than been heard but felt and remembered. It's a journey towards creating talks that leave a lasting impact on your audience.

The Path to Impactful Speaking

Impactful speaking is rooted in purpose and clarity. It goes beyond just delivering a message; it's about ensuring that your message carries weight, meaning, and relevance. Have you ever listened to a speech that not only informed you but also moved you? That's the power of purpose-driven communication.

Integrating Your Message with Audience Needs

The essence of crafting an impactful message lies in aligning your purpose with the needs and aspirations of your audience. It's about understanding what resonates with them and integrating it into your core message. When was the last time you tailored your message to

63

deeply connect with your listener's core desires?

The Art of Clear and Concise Messaging

Clarity and conciseness are key. A message that is clear and to the point is more likely to be understood and remembered. It's about distilling your message into its most potent form. How can you express your key points in a way that is both straightforward and powerful?

Practical Exercise: The Message Refinement

Let's engage in a practical exercise: the message refinement. Take a piece of your talk or a key message you wish to convey. Now, refine it. Strip it down to its most essential elements without losing its core meaning. How does this refined message differ in impact compared to its original form?

Reflecting On the Truth

As we wrap up this chapter, think about how the fourth noble truth guides us in crafting messages that are impactful and memorable. It's about being purposeful, clear, and empathetic in our communication, ensuring that every word we speak carries the weight of our wholesome intent.

NOTES

_____

_____

_____

_____

_____

_____

_____

_____

_____

_____

_____

_____

_____

_____

_____

_____

_____

_____

_____

_____

_____

_____

_____

_____

_____

_____

_____

_____

_____

_____

_____

_____

_____

_____

_____

_____

_____

_____

_____

_____

_____

Chapter 8: Wise Understanding - Deepening Your Grasp on Topic and Audience

Continuing Our Engaging Dialogue

As we comfortably settle into the next phase of our journey, envision us sharing a space of exploration and insight. This chapter invites us to delve into the concept of wise understanding, a crucial element in enhancing your public speaking skills.

Embracing Wise Understanding

Wise understanding, in the context of public speaking, is about gaining a profound and insightful grasp of both your topic and your audience. It's a journey that goes beyond surface-level knowledge, diving deep into the heart of what you are speaking about and to whom you are speaking.

Understanding Your Topic

To speak effectively, you must understand your topic not been intellectual alone but emotionally and contextually. It's about seeing the bigger picture and the finer details. How often do you find yourself engaged in a topic that you've explored from multiple angles and depths?

Connecting with your Audience

Similarly, understanding your audience is more than knowing their demographic. It's about comprehending their perspectives, challenges, and expectations. When was the last time you adjusted your speech based on a deeper understanding of your audience's background and needs?

The Art of Research and Empathy

Achieving wise understanding involves thorough research and a strong sense of empathy. It's a combination of hard facts and emotional intelligence. How do you balance these two in your preparation for a speech?

Practical Exercise: Dual Deep Dive

For our practical exercise, let's do a Dual Deep Dive. Choose a topic and spend some time researching it thoroughly. Then, put yourself in the shoes of your intended audience and see the topic from their perspective. How does this dual perspective enhance your understanding and potential delivery of the topic?

Reflecting On the Truth

As we conclude this chapter, consider the power of wise understanding to transform how you communicate. It's about having a rich, multi-dimensional grasp of both your subject matter and the people you are addressing.

NOTES

_____

_____

_____

_____

_____

_____

_____

_____

_____

_____

_____

_____

_____

_____

_____

_____

_____

_____

_____

_____

_____

_____

Chapter 9: Wise Intent - Aligning Your Purpose with Your Speaking Goals

Deepening Our Heart-to-Heart Conversation

As we progress in our journey, imagine us once again in our shared space of discovery and understanding. In this chapter, we'll explore the concept of wise intent and its crucial role in aligning your inner purpose with your speaking goals.

The Essence of Wise Intent

Wise intention, in the realm of public speaking, is about consciously aligning your deeper intentions with the goals of your speech. It's not simply about what you want to say, but also about why you want to say it and the impact you wish to create.

Understanding Your Inner Motivations

Before we can effectively communicate with others, we need to be clear about our own motivations. What drives you to speak? Is it to inform, to inspire, to persuade, or to connect? Reflect on a moment when your intent was perfectly aligned with your message. How did it influence the outcome?

The Power of Purposeful Speaking

When your speech is driven by a purpose that resonates deeply with you, it transcends mere words. Your audience can feel the authenticity and conviction in your voice. Have you ever been moved by a speaker whose passion and intent were unmistakably evident?

Aligning Intent with Audience Needs

Wise intent also involves aligning your goals with the needs and expectations of your audience. It's a harmonious balance between what you want to convey and what your audience needs to hear. How do you ensure your speaking intentions meet your audience's interests?

Practical Exercise: The Intent Alignment

Let's engage in a practical exercise called Intent Alignment. Think about an upcoming speaking engagement or talk you would love to deliver. Make three columns. Column one lists your core intention for this speech. Then, in column three, list down what you believe are the needs and expectations of your audience. In the middle column, write down how you can align these two aspects to enhance the effectiveness of your talk.

Reflecting On the Truth

As this chapter ends, ponder the significance of wise intent in your public speaking endeavours. It's about infusing every word with purpose and ensuring that your message as well reaches the ears but also touches the hearts of your audience.

NOTES

_____

_____

_____

_____

_____

_____

_____

_____

_____

_____

_____

_____

_____

_____

_____

_____

_____

_____

_____

_____

Chapter 10: Wise Speech - Mastering Clarity and Impact in Your Words

Continuing Our Engaging Exchange

As we reconvene in our shared space of exploration, let's delve into another vital aspect of our journey. In this chapter, we focus on wise speech and its significance in achieving clarity and impact in our communication.

The Art of Wise Speech

Wise speech in public speaking is about choosing words that are clear, truthful, and beneficial. It's about communicating in a way that is both understandable and resonant. Think about a time when someone's words deeply impacted you. What made their speech so powerful?

Clarity and Precision

The clarity of your speech is fundamental. It matters how you say things as much as what you say. Clear communication means using language that your audience can easily comprehend and relate to. How do you currently ensure that your speech is clear and concise?

Speaking Truthfully and Constructively

Wise speech also involves being truthful and constructive. It's about being honest in your communication, but also about ensuring that your words are helpful and uplifting. Have you experienced a situation where honest yet constructive speech made a difference?

The Power of Positive Language

The words you choose have the power to shape your audience's perception. Using positive, affirming language can create an encouraging and motivating atmosphere. How do you incorporate positivity into your language while maintaining authenticity?

Practical Exercise: The Clarity Check

Let's engage in a practical exercise called the Clarity Check. Take a section of your talk and review it. Are there any complex words or phrases that could be simplified? Is your message direct and easy to understand? Rewrite it with a focus on clarity and see how it transforms your message.

Reflecting On the Truth

As we wrap up this chapter, reflect on the importance of wise speech in your public speaking. Remember, the words you choose and the way you deliver them can profoundly influence your audience. It's about being heard; it's about being understood and remembered.

NOTES

_____

_____

_____

_____

_____

_____

_____

_____

_____

_____

_____

_____

_____

_____

_____

_____

_____

_____

_____

_____

Chapter 11: Wise Action - The Path to Mastering the Art of Speaking

Engaging in Our Meaningful Dialogue
As we continue our journey together, let's settle into our familiar, contemplative space. This chapter is dedicated to exploring wise action and how it plays a crucial role in practicing and perfecting the art of speaking.

Embracing Wise Action in Public Speaking
Wise action, in the realm of public speaking, is about taking deliberate, thoughtful steps towards honing your craft. It's not about what you do on stage only, but also what you do off it. How often do you consciously practice and refine your speaking skills?

The Practice of Deliberate Speaking

Just like any art, speaking requires practice. But merely any practice—wholesome practice. This means focusing on specific aspects of your speaking, seeking feedback, and continually challenging yourself to improve. When was the last time you expanded your comfort zone in a speaking scenario?

The Power of Consistent Effort

Consistency is key to mastering speaking. It's about regularly dedicating time to practice, whether it's rehearsing your speech, working on your vocal delivery, or refining your body language. How do you maintain a regular practice routine?

Reflective Learning and Feedback

Wise action also involves reflective learning and seeking constructive feedback. After each speaking engagement or conversation, take time to reflect on what went well and what could be improved. How often do you seek feedback from trusted colleagues, mentors, or your audience?

Practical Exercise: The Speaking Action Plan

Let's engage in a practical exercise: the Speaking Action Plan. Create a plan for your speaking practice for the next month. Set specific goals (e.g., improving storytelling, enhancing vocal variety), and outline the actions you'll take to achieve these goals. Remember, the plan should be realistic and achievable.

Reflecting On the Truth

As this chapter concludes, think about how incorporating wise action into your routine can significantly elevate your speaking abilities. It's about being methodical, consistent, and proactive in your approach to speaking.

NOTES

_____

_____

_____

_____

_____

_____

_____

_____

_____

_____

_____

_____

_____

_____

_____

_____

_____

_____

_____

_____

_____

_____

_____

_____

_____

_____

_____

_____

_____

_____

_____

_____

_____

_____

_____

_____

_____

_____

Chapter 12: Wise Livelihood - Contributing Positively Through Public Speaking

Nurturing Our Ongoing Conversation

As we reconvene in our journey of discovery and growth, let's delve into the concept of wise livelihood in the context of public speaking. This chapter explores how the art of speaking can be used as a source of strength for positive contributions in the world.

Understanding Wise Livelihood in Speaking

Wise livelihood, when applied to public speaking, is about using your voice and platform to make a positive impact. It's about ensuring that your speaking engagements align with values that contribute to the greater good. Think about a speech that in the same way informed you but also inspired you to make a positive change.

The Responsibility of the Speaker

As a speaker, you hold a significant responsibility. The words you choose and the messages you convey can influence thoughts, inspire actions, and even shape societies. How do you ensure that your speeches reflect responsible and ethical values?

Speaking for Positive Change

The essence of wise livelihood in speaking is to use your platform to advocate for positive change. This could mean raising awareness about important issues, inspiring action towards social causes, or simply spreading positivity and encouragement. What causes or values are you passionate about conveying in your speeches?

Aligning Passion with Purpose

Finding the intersection between what you're passionate about and what serves the greater good is key. It's about aligning your personal interests with messages that have a wider positive impact. How do you find balance between speaking about what you love and what serves others?

Practical Exercise: The Impact Analysis

Let's engage in a practical exercise: the impact analysis. Think about a topic you're planning to speak on. Analyse its potential impact: How does it serve your audience? How does it contribute positively to your community or society? This analysis can help refine your message to ensure it aligns with the principles of wise livelihood.

Reflecting On the Truth

As this chapter ends, ponder how your role as a speaker can extend beyond the stage. Wise Livelihood is about making your public speaking a vehicle for positive change, ensuring that your words not only resonate but also contribute to a better world.

NOTES

_____

_____

_____

_____

_____

_____

_____

_____

_____

_____

_____

_____

_____

_____

_____

_____

_____

_____

_____

_____

_____

_____

_____

_____

_____

_____

_____

_____

_____

_____

_____

_____

_____

_____

_____

_____

_____

_____

_____

_____

_____

_____

_____

_____

Chapter 13: Wise Effort - Cultivating Consistency and Persistence in Speaking Skills

Deepening Our Heartfelt Exchange

As we gather once more in our shared space of growth and understanding, let's explore the concept of wise effort in public speaking. This chapter is about the importance of consistent and persistent effort in honing your speaking skills.

Embracing Wise Effort in Public Speaking

Wise effort, in the context of public speaking, is about applying consistent and focused energy towards improving your skills. It's not about sporadic bursts of practice but a steady, enduring commitment. Reflect on how your speaking skills have evolved. Can you trace this progress back to specific, consistent efforts?

The Role of Persistence

Persistence is key to mastering any skill, especially public speaking. It involves pushing through challenges, setbacks, and even moments of self-doubt. Remember a time when you felt like giving up on speaking but persisted? What kept you going?

Consistency over Intensity

While intense practice sessions have their place, it's the regular, consistent efforts that lead to long-term improvement. Consistency in practicing your speeches, refining your techniques, and seeking feedback contributes to gradual but significant growth. How do you incorporate speaking practice into your regular routine?

Overcoming Plateaus with Wise Effort

Every speaker encounters plateaus in their journey. Wise Effort is about recognising these plateaus and strategically working to overcome them, whether it's by adapting your speaking styles, seeking new sources of inspiration, or experimenting with different content. What strategies do you use to overcome plateaus in your speaking skills?

Practical Exercise: The Consistency Challenge

Let's engage in a practical exercise called the Consistency Challenge. Set a small, achievable speaking-related goal for the next week (e.g., practicing a new vocal exercise daily or writing a short speech on a new topic). The focus here is on daily, consistent action, no matter how small.

Reflecting On the Truth

As this chapter concludes, think about how incorporating wise effort into your speaking journey can lead to profound improvements. Remember, it's really about the wisdom in how and where you apply it.

NOTES

_____

_____

_____

_____

_____

_____

_____

_____

_____

_____

_____

_____

_____

_____

_____

_____

_____

_____

_____

_____

_____

_____

_____

_____

_____

_____

_____

_____

_____

_____

_____

_____

_____

_____

_____

_____

_____

_____

_____

_____

_____

Chapter 14: Wise Mindfulness - Staying Present and Connected with Your Audience

Continuing our Intimate Conversation

Let's come together again in our journey of discovery, this time to explore the concept of wise mindfulness in the context of public speaking. In this chapter, we delve into the art of staying present and deeply connected with our audience.

Embracing Wise Mindfulness in Speaking

Wise mindfulness, in the sphere of public speaking, is about being fully present in the moment and acutely aware of yourself, your message, and your audience. It's about creating a space where you and your audience are engaged in a mutual, dynamic exchange.

Think back to a speaking experience where you felt completely in sync with your audience. What was different about that experience?

The Power of Presence

Being present while speaking is more than just being physically there; it's about being mentally and emotionally attuned. It means being aware of your thoughts, your feelings, and how your words are being received. How often do you find your mind wandering during a speech, and how do you bring it back?

Connecting With your Audience

Mindfulness helps create a deeper connection with your audience. It's about noticing the subtle cues—the nods, the smiles, the puzzled expressions—and adjusting your message accordingly. How do you ensure that you are merely speaking to your audience but also speaking with them?

The Practice of Mindful Speaking

Mindful speaking is a practice. It involves preparing not only your speech but also your mind. It's about centring yourself before you step onto the stage, taking deep breaths, and grounding yourself in the present moment. Do you have a pre-speech routine that helps you focus and calm your mind?

Practical Exercise: Mindful Speaking Moment

Let's engage in a practical exercise: mindful speaking moment. Next time you prepare for a speech, take a few minutes beforehand to practice mindfulness. Pay attention to your breathing while objectively observing your thoughts. Anchor yourself in the now by staying focused on your breath. Notice how this affects your delivery and connection with the audience.

Reflecting On the Truth

As we close this chapter, reflect on the importance of wise mindfulness in enhancing your public speaking. It's about being present in every word, every gesture, and every glance, creating a speaking experience that is beyond been informative but also deeply engaging and authentic.

NOTES

_____

_____

_____

_____

_____

_____

_____

_____

_____

_____

_____

_____

_____

_____

_____

_____

_____

_____

_____

_____

_____

_____

_____

_____

_____

_____

_____

_____

_____

_____

_____

_____

_____

_____

_____

_____

_____

_____

_____

Chapter 15: Wise Concentration - Channelling Your Energies for Effective Delivery

Engaging in Our Deepening Dialogue

As we gather once again in our shared space of learning and reflection, let's delve into the concept of wise concentration in public speaking. This chapter focuses on the importance of channelling your energies and attention for a truly effective delivery.

Understanding Wise Concentration

Wise concentration, in the art of public speaking, is about honing your focus and directing your mental and emotional energies towards your speech. It's the practice of being wholly absorbed in the moment of delivery, ensuring that every word and gesture is deliberate and impactful. Have you ever experienced a moment when you were completely absorbed in your speech, almost oblivious to distractions?

The Essence of Focused Energy

The ability to concentrate deeply while speaking is a skill that elevates your delivery. It's about filtering out distractions and channelling your mental energies towards your message and your audience. How do you usually manage distractions during a speech?

Balancing Preparation and Spontaneity

Wise concentration also involves striking a balance between thorough preparation and spontaneous engagement. While being well-prepared is essential, being overly scripted can hinder the natural flow of interaction. How do you balance preparation with the ability to be spontaneous and responsive?

Techniques for Enhancing Concentration

There are various techniques to enhance concentration, such as mindfulness practices, breathing exercises, and visualisation techniques. These practices can help calm your mind, sharpen your focus, and improve your presence on stage. What techniques do you use to enhance your concentration before and during a speech?

Practical Exercise: The Focus Drill

Let's engage in a practical exercise called the Focus Drill. Choose a topic and spend a few minutes speaking about it. During this exercise, whenever you notice your mind wandering, gently bring your focus back to your topic. This drill helps in developing the skill of redirecting your attention back to your speech.

Reflecting On the Truth

As we conclude this chapter, think about how wise concentration can transform your public speaking. It's about being mentally present and fully engaged with your speech, ensuring that your delivery is as effective and impactful as possible.

NOTES

_____

_____

_____

_____

_____

_____

_____

_____

_____

_____

_____

_____

_____

_____

_____

_____

_____

_____

Chapter 16: The Principle of Respect - Embracing Integrity and Compassion in Communication

Deepening Our Engaged Dialogue

As we reconvene in our ongoing conversation, let's explore a fundamental aspect of effective speaking: the principle of respect. Picture us delving into this topic not merely as a concept but as a living, breathing part of our communication.

The Essence of Respect in Communication

Respect in public speaking is about more than courtesy; it's about integrity and compassion. It involves honouring beyond only your audience's time and presence but also their diverse perspectives and experiences. Can you recall a time when you felt deeply respected as an audience member? What made that experience stand out?

Integrity: The Core of Respectful Speaking
Integrity is the backbone of respect. It means aligning your words with your values, ensuring honesty and authenticity in your message. It's about being true to yourself and to your audience. How do you ensure that your speeches reflect your true beliefs and values?

Compassion: Connecting Heart to Heart
Compassion in speaking is about empathetically connecting with your audience. It's understanding their needs, fears, and aspirations and addressing them in your speech. How often do you find yourself truly empathising with your audience, seeing things from their perspective?

The Power of Listening

Active listening is a significant aspect of respect. It's about genuinely paying attention to your audience's reactions and feedback and transforming the way you speak to be more responsive and considerate. What strategies do you use to ensure you are actively listening to your audience?

Practical Exercise: The Respect Audit

This practical exercise called the Respect Audit, reflect on your last speech or presentation. Ask yourself: Did I treat my audience with respect? Did I speak with integrity and compassion? How can I improve in these areas for my next speech? This reflection can guide you in making your future communications more respectful and impactful.

Reflecting On the Truth

As we conclude this chapter, think about how the principle of respect can transform your public speaking. It's not simply about what you say, it's about how you say it and the intent behind it. Respect, integrity, and compassion can elevate your speaking from mere words to a meaningful, heartfelt connection.

NOTES

_____

_____

_____

_____

_____

_____

_____

_____

_____

_____

_____

_____

_____

_____

_____

_____

_____

_____

_____

Chapter 17: The Principle of Honesty - Valuing Authenticity and Trust in Public Speaking

Deepening Our Meaningful Conversation

As we continue our shared journey, let's turn our focus to a cornerstone of effective communication: the principle of honesty. Imagine us discussing this not as a distant concept but as a vital, living principle in every word we speak.

The Power of Honesty in Speaking

Honesty in public speaking is about more than just not lying; it's about being authentic, genuine, and true to your values. Establishing a foundation of trust with your audience is crucial. Can you think of a time when a speaker's authenticity deeply resonated with you? What impact did it have?

Authenticity: Heart of Honest Communication
Authenticity is the soul of honesty. It means your words are a true reflection of your beliefs and intentions. It's about being the same person on stage as you are off stage. How do you ensure that your public persona aligns with your true self?

Building Trust with your audience
When your audience trusts you, they are more open to your message, more forgiving of mistakes, and more receptive to your ideas. Trust is a critical outcome of honest communication. What steps do you take to build and maintain trust with your audience?

Overcoming the Temptation to Exaggerate

One of the challenges in public speaking is resisting the urge to embellish or exaggerate to make a point. True honesty involves having the courage to speak plainly and truthfully, even when it's tempting to stretch the truth. How do you handle situations where there's pressure to embellish your message?

Practical Exercise: The Authenticity Check

As a practical exercise (the authenticity check), record your next speech or practice session. Then, watch it and ask yourself: Was I being genuinely honest and authentic? Did my words truly reflect my beliefs and values? This exercise can help you align your speaking more closely with the principle of honesty.

Reflecting On the Truth

As we end this chapter, consider the profound impact that honesty and authenticity can have on your effectiveness as a speaker. Honesty isn't just about factual accuracy; it's about being true to yourself and forging a genuine connection with your audience through trust and authenticity.

NOTES

_____

_____

_____

_____

_____

_____

_____

_____

_____

_____

_____

_____

_____

_____

_____

_____

_____

_____

_____

_____

_____

_____

_____

_____

_____

_____

_____

_____

_____

_____

_____

_____

_____

_____

_____

_____

_____

_____

Chapter 18: The Principle of Mindfulness - Navigating Boundaries and Ethics in Expression

Engaging in a Purposeful Dialogue

As we gather once again in our journey of exploration, let's focus on a crucial aspect of effective communication: the principle of truthful expression. Envision this chapter as a heart-to-heart conversation about the power of truth in our words.

The Essence of Truthful Expression

Truthful expression is more than just factual accuracy; it's about conveying your message with clarity and honesty. It involves aligning your words with wholesome true intentions and beliefs. Think about a time when a speaker's truthfulness profoundly impacted you. What made their message so powerful?

Clarity in Communication

Clarity is the cornerstone of truthful expression. It makes your message understandable and free from ambiguity or deception. How do you ensure that your speeches are clear and accurately convey your intended message?

The Positive Impact of Truth

Speaking truthfully is ethically right which has a wholesome impact on your audience. The truth builds trust and fosters a genuine connection. Can you recall an instance were speaking the truth, though challenging, had a positive outcome?

Navigating Difficult Truths

The challenge with truthful expression is navigating difficult truths—those that might be hard to say or hard for the audience to hear. How do you balance being honest yet being caring to your audience's feelings and reactions?

Practical Exercise: The Truth Alignment

As a practical exercise, review a recent piece of communication you delivered. Reflect on whether your words were in complete alignment with the truth. Were there areas where clarity could be improved? This exercise can help refine your ability to express truthfully and clearly.

Reflecting On the Truth

As we conclude this chapter, consider the role of truthful expression in enhancing your effectiveness as a speaker. Remember, truth in communication is not solely about the words you choose; it's about the congruence between your words, your intentions, and your actions.

NOTES

_____

_____

_____

_____

_____

_____

_____

_____

_____

_____

_____

_____

_____

_____

_____

_____

_____

_____

_____

_____

Chapter 19: The Principle of Truthful Expression - Fostering Clarity and Positive Impact through Words

Engaging in a Purposeful Dialogue

As we gather once again in our journey of exploration, let's focus on a crucial aspect of effective communication: the principle of truthful expression. Envision this beyond a chapter but as a heart-to-heart conversation about the power of truth in our words.

The Essence of Truthful Expression

Truthful expression in public speaking is more than just factual accuracy; it's about conveying your message with clarity and honesty. It involves aligning your words with your true intentions and beliefs. Think about a time when a speaker's truthfulness profoundly impacted you. What made their message so powerful?

Clarity in Communication

Clarity is the cornerstone of truthful expression. It's about making your message understandable and free from ambiguity or deception. How do you ensure that your speeches are clear and accurately convey your intended message?

The Positive Impact of Truth

Speaking truthfully isn't just ethically right; it also has a positive impact on your audience. The truth builds trust and fosters a genuine connection. Can you recall an instance were speaking the truth, though challenging, had a positive outcome?

Navigating Difficult Truths

One of the challenges of truthful expression is navigating difficult truths—those that might be hard to say or hard for the audience to hear. How do you balance being honest with being sensitive to your audience's feelings and reactions?

Practical Exercise: The Truth Alignment

As a practical exercise, review a recent speech or piece of communication you've delivered. Reflect on whether your words were in complete alignment with your truth. Were there areas where clarity could be improved? This exercise can help refine your ability to express yourself truthfully and clearly.

Reflecting On the Truth

As we conclude this chapter, consider the role of truthful expression in enhancing your effectiveness as a speaker. Remember, truth in communication is not really about the words you choose; it's about congruence between your words, your intentions, and your actions.

NOTES

_____

_____

_____

_____

_____

_____

_____

_____

_____

_____

_____

_____

_____

_____

_____

_____

_____

_____

Chapter 20: The Principle of Clear Mindfulness - Enhancing Focus and Presence in Speaking

Engaging in Our Insightful Exchange

As we meet again in our shared journey of communication, let's explore the principle of clear mindfulness. Picture this as a meaningful, interactive discussion about how mindfulness can enhance your focus and presence in public speaking.

The Essence of Clear Mindfulness in Speaking

Clear mindfulness in public speaking is about being fully present, both mentally and emotionally, during your speech. It's about having a heightened awareness of yourself, your message, and how it resonates with your audience. Reflect on a speaking experience where you felt completely 'in the zone'. What elements contributed to that sense of presence and focus?

Cultivating Presence on Stage

Presence is the heart of clear mindfulness. It's not merely about physically standing on the stage; it's about being wholly engaged with your audience and your message. How do you prepare yourself to be fully present and focused during your speeches?

Mindfulness as a Tool for Focus

In a world of constant distractions, maintaining focus during public speaking can be challenging. Mindfulness practices can help centre your thoughts and keep you grounded in the moment. What mindfulness techniques do you use to enhance your concentration while speaking?

Overcoming Nervousness with Mindfulness

Nervousness is a common challenge for speakers. Clear mindfulness can help you acknowledge and manage these feelings, transforming them into positive energy for your speech. How do you use mindfulness to handle nerves before and during your presentations?

Practical Exercise: Mindfulness Breathing

This practical exercise, the Mindfulness Breathing, do this before your next speech: Take a few moments to focus solely on your breath. Deep, slow breaths that go below your belly button can help calm your mind and sharpen your focus. Observe how this simple practice affects your presence and clarity in your next speaking engagement.

Reflecting On the Truth

As we wrap up this chapter, think about how the principle of clear mindfulness can significantly enhance your public speaking. It's about more than just delivering a speech; it's about connecting deeply with your message and your audience, creating a more impactful and memorable experience.

NOTES

_____

_____

_____

_____

_____

_____

_____

_____

_____

_____

_____

_____

_____

_____

_____

_____

_____

_____

_____

_____

_____

_____

_____

_____

_____

_____

_____

_____

_____

_____

_____

_____

_____

_____

_____

_____

_____

_____

_____

_____

_____

Chapter 21: Embracing Change - The Inevitability of Evolution - Adapting to the Ever-Changing Landscape of Public Speaking

Engaging in a Dynamic Conversation

As we continue our enriching dialogue, let's turn our attention to a vital aspect of public speaking: the inevitability of change and evolution in the field. Imagine us exploring this not as a theoretical concept only but as a practical, ever-present reality in our speaking endeavours.

The Nature of Change in Public Speaking

In public speaking, change is constant. It's in the evolving audience expectations, the shifting trends in communication, and the continuous advancement of technology. Reflect on how public speaking has evolved over the years. How have these changes impacted your approach to speaking?

Adapting to New Audiences and Formats
Adaptability is key to navigating the changing landscape. It involves understanding and connecting with diverse audiences and being comfortable with various speaking formats, from in-person to digital platforms. How do you stay flexible and adaptable in your speaking style?

The Role of Lifelong Learning
Embracing change in public speaking also means committing to lifelong learning. It's about continuously updating your skills, being open to new ideas, and incorporating fresh perspectives into your speeches. What learning practices do you engage in to keep your speaking skills sharp and relevant?

Keeping Up with Technological Advancements
Technology has dramatically transformed the way we communicate. Staying abreast of these changes and leveraging new tools can enhance your effectiveness as a speaker. How do you incorporate technology into your speaking practice?

Practical Exercise: Adaptation Reflection
This practical exercise, Adaptation Reflection, think about a recent change in the public speaking landscape (e.g., virtual speaking, new audience demographics). Reflect on how you adapted (or could adapt) to this change. Consider what new strategies or skills you could adopt to stay relevant and effective.

Reflecting On the Truth

As we conclude this chapter, ponder the importance of embracing change in your public speaking journey. It's about more than just keeping up; it's about thriving in an ever-evolving environment, using change as a catalyst for growth and improvement in your communication skills.

NOTES

_____

_____

_____

_____

_____

_____

_____

_____

_____

_____

_____

_____

_____

_____

_____

_____

_____

_____

_____

_____

_____

_____

_____

_____

_____

_____

_____

_____

_____

_____

_____

_____

_____

_____

_____

_____

_____

_____

_____

_____

_____

_____

Chapter 22: Resilience in Adversity - Navigating Challenges - Finding Strength and Growth in Speaking Despite Obstacles

Engaging in an Empowering Discussion

As we come together once again in our journey of discovery, let's focus on a crucial aspect of public speaking: resilience in the face of adversity. Imagine us having a deep and meaningful conversation about overcoming challenges and growing stronger as speakers.

The Reality of Challenges in Public Speaking

Every speaker, regardless of their experience or skill level, faces challenges. These might be external, like difficult audiences or technical issues, or internal, such as self-doubt or anxiety. Can you recall a time when you faced a significant challenge in your speech? What was that experience like?

From Resilience to Antifragile

Resilience is about more than enduring difficulties; it's about learning from them and growing from them. It involves maintaining your composure, adapting your approach, and emerging stronger. How do you cultivate resilience in your speaking practice?

In public speaking, moving from resilience to antifragility means not enduring the stresses of speaking only but growing stronger from them, turning challenges into opportunities for improvement. How can embracing this concept transform your approach to public speaking?

Turning Obstacles into Opportunities

Every challenge in public speaking is an opportunity for growth. It's about shifting your perspective to see obstacles as stepping-stones rather than roadblocks. How have you transformed a speaking challenge into an opportunity in the past?

The Power of Preparation and Practice

Preparation and practice are key to moving from resilience to antifragility. They equip you with the tools and confidence to handle unexpected situations. What are your strategies for preparing and practicing your speeches to build your resilience, thus becoming antifragile?

Practical Exercise: The Challenge of Reflection

The practical exercise called, The Challenge Reflection, think about a recent obstacle you encountered in your public speaking. Reflect on how you addressed it and what you learned from the experience. Consider how you could apply these learnings to future speaking engagements to enhance yourself, thus moving from resilience to antifragility.

Reflecting On the Truth

As we close this chapter, think about the role of resilience in your public speaking journey. It's about embracing challenges, learning from them, and using them to strengthen your skills and confidence. Resilience is not about surviving adversity; it's about thriving and growing through every speaking experience.

NOTES

_____

_____

_____

_____

_____

_____

_____

_____

_____

_____

_____

_____

_____

_____

_____

_____

_____

_____

_____

_____

Chapter 23: Each Second is Once in a Lifetime - Valuing Each Speech - Understanding the Impermanence and Impact of Every Speaking Opportunity

Engaging in a Reflective Dialogue

As we reconvene in our ongoing exploration of public speaking, let's delve into the concept that each speech is once in a lifetime and the value of each speech. Imagine us discussing this in a thoughtful, introspective manner, recognising the fleeting yet significant nature of every speaking opportunity.

The Impermanence of Speaking Opportunities

Each time you speak, it's a unique, unrepeatable moment. Whether it's a formal presentation, a casual talk, or an impromptu speech, each opportunity carries its own significance. Reflect on a memorable speaking experience. What made it unique, and how did you embrace that moment?

Valuing Every Speaking Experience
Understanding the impermanence of speaking opportunities encourages us to value each one. It's about giving your best, being fully present, and appreciating the chance to share your message. How do you ensure that you fully engage with and value each speaking opportunity?

The Lasting Impact of Fleeting Moments
Though speaking moments are transient, their impact can be long-lasting. The words you choose, the emotions you convey, and the connections you make can resonate with your audience long after the speech ends. Have you

ever realised the lasting impact of a particular speech you delivered?

Embracing the Present in Public Speaking

Being fully present during a speech means more than just delivering words; it's about connecting authentically with your audience, being attuned to their reactions, and adapting your message in real time. What techniques do you use to stay present and connected during your speeches?

Practical Exercise: The Moment Reflection

A practical exercise called Moment Reflection, think back to your last talk or conversation. Reflect on how you engaged with that moment. Were you fully present? Did you value the opportunity? Consider what you might do differently next time to enhance your presence and the impact of your interaction.

Reflecting On the Truth

As we conclude this chapter, ponder the transient yet powerful nature of each speaking opportunity. Embracing the finality of these moments encourages us to give our best, connect deeply, and leave a lasting impression. Each speech, no matter how brief, is an opportunity to make a meaningful impact.

NOTES

_____

_____

_____

_____

_____

_____

_____

_____

_____

_____

_____

_____

_____

_____

_____

_____

_____

_____

_____

_____

_____

_____

_____

_____

_____

_____

_____

_____

_____

_____

_____

_____

_____

_____

_____

_____

_____

_____

_____

_____

_____

Chapter 24: Cherishing Connections - The Transience of Relationships - Building and Appreciating Relationships in the Realm of Public Speaking

Engaging in a Heartfelt Conversation

As we gather again in our journey of exploration and growth, let's focus on how temporary but valuable relationships are in public speaking. Picture us engaging in a deep, meaningful dialogue about how we build and cherish these connections, understanding their fleeting yet significant nature.

Impermanent Nature of Speaking Relationships

In public speaking, relationships with your listener, co-speakers, and even organisers are often transient. Each interaction, though brief, holds potential for significant impact. Think about a meaningful connection you made through speaking. What made it memorable, despite its brief nature?

Valuing Every Interaction

Understanding the transient nature of these relationships encourages us to value every interaction. Whether it's a short conversation after a speech or a quick exchange before a presentation, each moment is an opportunity to connect and leave a lasting impression. How do you ensure that you make the most of these fleeting interactions?

Building Lasting Impressions

The art of public speaking allows us to create lasting impressions that transcend the transience of the interaction. It's about the words you say, the emotions you share, and the genuine interest you show in your audience. What strategies do you employ to create lasting impressions through your brief interactions?

Appreciating the Momentary Bonds

Each speaking opportunity allows you to form momentary bonds with your audience. Cherishing these connections means being fully present, empathetic, and engaging. How do you foster a sense of connection and appreciation with your audience, even in brief encounters?

Practical Exercise: The Connection Reflection

A practical exercise called; The Connection Reflection recalls your last communication. Reflect on the interactions you had. Were you fully present in those moments? How did you acknowledge and appreciate those brief connections? Think about ways you can deepen your engagement in future interactions.

Reflecting On the Truth

As we close this chapter, reflect on the importance of cherishing the transient relationships we form in public speaking. Each interaction, no matter how brief, is an opportunity to build connections, share experiences, and impact lives. Remember, the value of these connections lies not in their duration but in the depth of the exchange.

NOTES

_____

_____

_____

_____

_____

_____

_____

_____

_____

_____

_____

_____

_____

_____

_____

_____

_____

_____

_____

_____

_____

_____

_____

_____

_____

_____

_____

_____

_____

_____

_____

_____

_____

_____

_____

_____

_____

_____

_____

_____

Chapter 25: The Foundation of Actions - Building Your Legacy - How Your Words and Deeds Shape Your Public Speaking Journey

Engaging in a Thought-Provoking Dialogue

As we meet once more on this enlightening journey, let's delve into the significant role of actions in shaping your legacy in public speaking. Imagine this conversation as an exploration of how every word you speak and action you take weaves the fabric of your lasting impact.

The Impact of Words and Actions

In public speaking, your words and actions are not fleeting; they build your legacy. Each speech and every interaction, no matter how small, contributes to the narrative of your speaking career. Reflect on how your past speeches have shaped your current standing. How have your words and actions defined you as a speaker?

Crafting Your Legacy Through Speech

Your legacy as a speaker is crafted through consistent, authentic, and impactful communication. It's about aligning your values with your message and delivering it with conviction. What message do you want to be known for, and how are you embedding this into your speeches?

Consistency in Words and Actions

Consistency between what you say and what you do is crucial. It builds credibility and trust. Think about a time when your actions didn't align with your words. What was the impact, and what did you learn from it?

The Power of Intentional Speaking

Intentional speaking involves being mindful of the long-term impact of your words. It's about understanding that your speeches can influence, inspire, and initiate change. How do you ensure that your speeches are purposeful and aligned with the legacy you want to build?

Practical Exercise: The Legacy Reflection

Practical exercises called, The Legacy Reflection, think about a recent speech, presentation, or communication. Reflect on the message you conveyed and the actions you took. Were they aligned with the legacy you wish to build? Consider how you can enhance the alignment between your words, actions, and the legacy you aspire to create.

Reflecting On the Truth

As we conclude this chapter, consider the enduring nature of your words and actions in public speaking. Your legacy is not a record of what you've done only, but a living testament to the impact you've had and will continue to have. Every word you speak and every action you take shapes the path of your speaking journey and the legacy you leave behind.

NOTES

_____

_____

_____

_____

_____

_____

_____

_____

_____

_____

_____

_____

_____

_____

_____

_____

_____

_____

_____

_____

_____

Chapter 26: The Art of Generosity in Speaking - Enriching Your Audience through Giving of Knowledge and Insight

Engaging in a Generous Exchange

As we come together once more in our journey, let's explore the concept of generosity in the realm of public speaking. Imagine this as a deep and meaningful conversation about the art of giving not simply information but wisdom and understanding to your audience.

Generosity Beyond Words

Generosity in speaking goes beyond the mere sharing of information. It's about offering your knowledge, insights, and experiences with a genuine desire to enrich your audience's lives.

Reflect on a time when you felt that a speaker was genuinely generous with their knowledge. How did that affect you?

The Gift of Understanding

True generosity in speaking involves striving to ensure that your audience understands and connects with your message. It's about tailoring your speech to meet their needs and level of comprehension. How do you adapt your speaking to ensure that your audience is receiving the full benefit of your knowledge?

Sharing Insights with Empathy

Empathy is a key aspect of generous speaking. It means being attuned to the audience's feelings and perspectives and sharing insights that resonate with them on a deeper level. How do you incorporate empathy into your approach to ensure your insights are both relevant and meaningful?

The Impact of Generous Speaking

When you speak generously, you create a lasting impact. Your audience leaves not with information alone, but also with knowledge that can inspire change or provide comfort. How do you measure the impact of your generosity in your speeches?

Practical Exercise: The Generosity Audit

This practical exercise called the Generosity Audit, review one of your recent speeches or presentations. Reflect on whether you were truly generous with your knowledge and insights. Did you offer understanding and empathy along with the information? Think about ways you can enhance your generosity in future speaking engagements.

Reflecting On the Truth

As we conclude this chapter, ponder the role of generosity in public speaking. Generosity is not uniquely about the quantity of information given; it's about the quality of understanding, insight, and connection you offer. It's a powerful way to enrich and engage your audience, leaving a lasting impression that extends far beyond the spoken word.

NOTES

_____

_____

_____

_____

_____

_____

_____

_____

_____

_____

_____

_____

_____

_____

_____

_____

_____

_____

_____

_____

_____

_____

_____

_____

_____

_____

_____

_____

_____

_____

_____

_____

_____

_____

_____

_____

_____

_____

_____

_____

_____

_____

_____

Chapter 27: The Ethics of Communication - Upholding Integrity and Respect in Every Word

Engaging in a Meaningful Dialogue

As we reconvene in our exploration of effective public speaking, let's delve into the crucial aspect of ethics in communication. Imagine us having a sincere and deep conversation about the importance of integrity and respect in every word we say.

The Foundation of Ethical Communication

Ethical communication is the bedrock of trust and credibility in public speaking. It involves being honest, transparent, and respectful in every interaction. Reflect on a moment when you witnessed or delivered a speech that exemplified ethical communication. What stood out about that experience?

Upholding Integrity

Integrity in speaking is about aligning your words with your values and beliefs. It's about being true to yourself and your message, ensuring that what you say is a genuine reflection of who you are and what you stand for. How do you ensure that your speeches reflect your personal and professional integrity?

The Importance of Respectful Speech

Respect in communication goes beyond polite words. It's about acknowledging the dignity of your audience, being mindful of sensitivities, and avoiding harmful or derogatory language. How do you practice respect in your speaking, especially when addressing challenging topics?

Navigating Ethical Dilemmas

Public speaking often presents ethical dilemmas, such as balancing honesty with diplomacy or handling sensitive information. How do you navigate these dilemmas while maintaining your ethical standards?

Practical Exercise: The Integrity Check

For a practical exercise called the Integrity Check, think about your most recent communication. Reflect on whether your words and delivery uphold your ethical standards. Were you honest, transparent, and respectful? Consider how you might enhance the ethical dimension of your communication in future engagements.

Reflecting On the Truth

As we wrap up this chapter, consider the profound impact of upholding ethics in your communication. Ethical speaking is not simply a professional standard; it's a commitment to honour the trust your audience places in you. It's about building a legacy of integrity and respect that goes beyond the podium.

NOTES

_____

_____

_____

_____

_____

_____

_____

_____

_____

_____

_____

_____

_____

_____

_____

_____

_____

_____

_____

_____

_____

_____

_____

_____

_____

_____

_____

_____

_____

_____

_____

_____

_____

_____

_____

_____

_____

_____

_____

_____

_____

_____

_____

_____

Chapter 28: The Power of Patience in Oratory - Cultivating Endurance and Understanding in Your Speaking Journey

Engaging in a Reflective Conversation

As we continue our dialogue on the art of public speaking, let's focus on a vital yet often overlooked aspect: the power of patience. Imagine this discussion as an exploration of how patience influences and enriches your journey as a speaker.

Understanding the Role of Patience

Patience in communication is more than just waiting for your turn to speak; it's about enduring challenges, persistently improving your skills, and empathetically engaging with your audience. Think about a time in your speaking journey where patience played a key role. What did that experience teach you?

Developing Patience in Practice

Patience is crucial to honing your oratory skills. It's about practicing repeatedly, refining your message, and accepting that improvement takes time. How do you practice patience in your preparations and rehearsals?

Patience with Your Audience

Understanding and patience with your audience are essential for effective communication. It involves adjusting your pace, clarifying your points, and being receptive to their feedback. How do you exercise patience when interacting with your audience, especially during Q&A sessions or discussions?

Overcoming Setbacks with Patience

Every speaker faces setbacks. Patience is key to overcoming these challenges without becoming discouraged. It's about viewing each setback as an opportunity to learn and grow. How do you maintain patience and resilience in the face of obstacles?

Practical Exercise: The Patience Reflection

The practical exercise, The Patience Reflection, recall a recent communication scenario where you felt impatient, either with yourself or your audience. Reflect on the situation and think about how a more patient approach could have altered the outcome. Use this reflection to identify ways you can cultivate more patience in your future speaking engagements.

Reflecting On the Truth

As we close this chapter, consider the profound impact that patience can have on your effectiveness as a speaker. Patience besides being a virtue is a practical tool that enhances your ability to communicate effectively, connect with your audience, and grow as a speaker. It's about embracing the journey with endurance, understanding, and a steady commitment to improvement.

NOTES

_____

_____

_____

_____

_____

_____

_____

_____

_____

_____

_____

_____

_____

_____

_____

_____

_____

_____

_____

_____

_____

_____

_____

_____

_____

_____

_____

_____

_____

_____

_____

_____

_____

_____

_____

_____

_____

_____

_____

_____

Chapter 29: The Drive for Excellence - Embracing Diligence and Passion in Perfecting Your Craft

Engaging in a Motivated Dialogue

As we reconvene in our enriching conversation about public speaking, let's turn our focus to the drive for excellence. This is not simply about diligence and passion in a general sense, but specifically how these qualities can elevate your craft of public speaking to new heights.

The Essence of Diligence in Speaking

Diligence in public speaking is about a consistent, dedicated effort to improve. It's about practicing even when it's convenient but as a regular discipline. Reflect on how a diligent approach has shaped your speaking skills. What changes have you noticed in your performance because of consistent practice?

Fuelling Your Speaking with Passion

Passion is the fire that drives excellence. It's what keeps you going when things get tough, and it's what makes your speeches come alive. How does your passion for your topics and for speaking itself come through in your presentations?

Perfecting Your Craft

The journey to excellence in public speaking is a continuous process of learning, practicing, and refining. It involves seeking feedback, learning from mistakes, and always aiming for a higher standard. What strategies do you use to continually perfect your speaking craft?

The Role of Persistence

Persistence is key to the drive for excellence. It's about not giving up when faced with challenges or when progress seems slow. How do you maintain your commitment to excellence, especially in the face of setbacks or plateaus in your development?

Practical Exercise: The Excellence Audit

For a practical exercise called The Excellence Audit, review a recording of one of your recent speeches. Look for areas were diligence and passion shine through, as well as areas for improvement. Think about how you can incorporate more of these qualities into your preparation and delivery.

Reflecting On the Truth

As we conclude this chapter, think about the importance of diligence and passion in your pursuit of excellence in public speaking. These qualities are not about achieving a high level of skill only; they're about inspiring your audience, leaving a lasting impact, and finding personal fulfilment in your craft.

NOTES

_____

_____

_____

_____

_____

_____

_____

_____

_____

_____

_____

_____

_____

_____

_____

_____

_____

_____

_____

_____

Chapter 30: The Focus of the Speaker - Harnessing Focus for Impactful and Engaging Speeches

Engaging in a Focused Discussion

As we meet again in our shared journey of public speaking, let's delve into the crucial aspect of focus. Imagine us having a deep, engaging conversation about the power of concentration to enhance the impact and engagement of your speeches.

The Role of Focus in Public Speaking

Focus on public speaking is about channelling your mental and emotional energy towards your message and your audience. It's the ability to be fully present, not physically alone, but with your entire being. Think back to a time when you were completely absorbed in a speech. What was the effect on your delivery and on your audience?

Cultivating Speaker Focus

Developing focus as a speaker involves more than just avoiding distractions; it's about creating a connection with your topic and your audience. It's about immersing yourself in the moment. How do you prepare yourself to be fully focused during your speeches?

Overcoming Barriers to Focus

Distractions and wandering thoughts are common challenges to maintaining focus. Addressing these barriers is key to ensuring your message is delivered with clarity and purpose. What techniques or practices do you use to overcome these challenges and maintain your concentration while speaking?

The Impact of Focused Speaking

When you speak with focus, your message becomes clearer, your engagement with the audience deepens, and your ability to persuade and inspire increases. How has focused speaking impacted your ability to connect with and influence your audience?

Practical Exercise: The Focus Practice

The practical exercise called the Focus Practice, during your next speech preparation; take a moment to centre yourself before practicing. Focus on your breath, clear your mind, and then deliver your speech with full concentration. Reflect on how this affects your delivery and connection with your audience.

Reflecting On the Truth

As we wrap up this chapter, consider the transformative power of focus in public speaking. Focus is more than a skill; it's a practice that elevates your speaking to new levels of clarity and engagement. It enables you to connect more deeply with your audience and to deliver your message with greater impact.

NOTES

_____

_____

_____

_____

_____

_____

_____

_____

_____

_____

_____

_____

_____

_____

_____

_____

_____

_____

_____

_____

_____

Chapter 31: The Wisdom of Words - Integrating Deep Understanding and Insight into Your Messages

Engaging in an Insightful Conversation

As we come together once more in our exploration of the art of public speaking, let's focus on a vital element: the wisdom of words. Picture us engaged in a profound discussion about how deep understanding and insight can be woven into the very fabric of your messages.

The Essence of Wisdom in Public Speaking

Wisdom in public speaking is more than just knowledge; it's the deep understanding and insightful application of that knowledge in your communication. It's about conveying your message in a way that reflects a deeper comprehension of the subject and its impact on the audience. Can you recall a speech where the speaker's wisdom transformed their message into something truly impactful?

Cultivating Depth in Your Messages

To infuse wisdom into your speeches, it's important to delve beyond surface-level information. This involves researching thoroughly, reflecting deeply on your topic, and understanding the broader implications of your message. How do you ensure that your communication is more informative but also insightful and thought-provoking?

Conveying Insights with Clarity

The true challenge lies in translating your insights into clear and understandable messages. It's about striking a balance between depth and accessibility, ensuring that your audience not only hears your words but also grasps their deeper meaning. How do you simplify complex ideas without losing their essence?

The Power of Thoughtful Word Choice

Choosing the right words is crucial to expressing wisdom. Each word should be selected for its ability to convey the exact nuance of your insight. How do you select words that resonate with your audience and enhance the depth of your message?

Practical Exercise: The Insight Integration

For a practical exercise called Insight Integration, take a key concept from your next talk and think deeply about its implications. Distil this insight into a clear, concise statement. During your speech, observe how this integrated insight resonates with your audience.

Reflecting On the Truth
As we conclude this chapter, think about the transformative power of integrating wisdom into your words. It's about more than sharing information; it's about enlightening your audience, offering them not just data but understanding and perspective. The wisdom of your words can leave a lasting impression, one that goes beyond the moment and stays with your audience long after your speech has ended.

NOTES

_____

_____

_____

_____

_____

_____

_____

_____

_____

_____

_____

_____

_____

_____

_____

_____

_____

_____

_____

_____

_____

Chapter 32: The Essence of Expression - Understanding Form in Speaking - Mastering the Physical Aspects of Communication

Deep Dynamic Conversation

As we gather again in our ongoing exploration of effective public speaking, let's delve into the physical aspect of communication—the essence of expression. Think of this as a conversation that goes beyond words, focusing on the way your body communicates.

The Role of Physical Expression

Physical expression in speaking involves more than just standing and delivering words. It's about how you use your entire body to convey your message. Your posture, gestures, and facial expressions all play a vital role. Reflect on a moment when a speaker's physical presence significantly enhanced their message. What made it so effective?

Mastering Posture and Gestures

Good posture and purposeful gestures are foundational to effective physical expression. They convey confidence and help emphasise your message. How do you ensure that your body language aligns with and supports what you're saying?

The Impact of Facial Expressions

Your facial expressions can communicate a spectrum of emotions and nuances that words alone cannot. They can engage, reassure, and connect with your audience. How aware are you of your facial expressions while speaking, and how do they affect your overall message?

The Power of Eye Contact

Eye contact is a powerful tool in public speaking. It helps establish a connection with your audience, making your communication more personal and impactful. What strategies do you use to maintain effective eye contact, especially in different speaking environments?

Practical Exercise: Physical Expression Drill

A practical exercise, Physical Expression Drill, record yourself delivering a speech, then watch it, focusing solely on your physical expression. Assess your posture, gestures, facial expressions, and eye contact. Are they enhancing your message or detracting from it? Use this reflection to improve your physical expression in future speeches.

Reflecting On the Truth

As we conclude this chapter, think about the significance of mastering the physical aspects of communication in public speaking. It's not just about what you say, but how your entire being says it. Effective physical expression can dramatically enhance the impact of your message, making it more memorable and engaging for your audience.

NOTES

_____

_____

_____

_____

_____

_____

_____

_____

_____

_____

_____

_____

_____

_____

_____

_____

_____

_____

_____

_____

_____

_____

_____

_____

Chapter 33: Navigating Sensations - The Impact of Feelings in Speech - Harnessing Emotions for Effective and Empathetic Communication

Engaging in an Emotionally Insightful Dialogue

As we reconvene in our exploration of public speaking, let's focus on the role of emotions and sensations in communication. Envision this as a deep and engaging conversation about how feelings, both yours and your audience's, play a crucial role in the effectiveness of your speeches.

The Power of Emotional Expression

Emotions in speaking are not by products of your message; they are an integral part of it. The way you express your feelings can profoundly impact how your message is received. Reflect on a communication that emotionally moved you. What was it about the speaker's emotional expression that touched you?

Taking Care of your emotions

Being aware of and managing your own emotions is key to effective communication. It involves recognising your feelings and channelling them to enhance your message, rather than letting them detract from it. How do you navigate your emotions during a speech?

Empathising with your Audience

Empathy in public speaking is about connecting with the emotional state of your audience. It's understanding their feelings and reflecting that understanding in your communication. How do you tune into your audience's emotions and adjust your speech accordingly?

Balancing Emotional Expression

Balancing emotional expression is crucial. Too little, and your speech may seem dispassionate; too much, and it might feel overwhelming. What strategies do you use to strike the right balance in emotional expression to enhance your communication?

Practical Exercise: Emotion Mapping

For a practical exercise called Emotion Mapping, select a portion of your next speech and map out the emotions you want to convey in each section. Practice delivering these parts with the intended emotional expression. Afterwards, reflect on how aligning specific emotions with your message affected the delivery and reception of your speech.

Reflecting On the Truth

As we conclude this chapter, consider the significant impact that understanding and harnessing emotions have on your effectiveness as a speaker. Emotions are a powerful tool in communication, capable of transforming your message into an experience that resonates deeply with your audience.

NOTES

_____

_____

_____

_____

_____

_____

_____

_____

_____

_____

_____

_____

_____

_____

_____

_____

_____

_____

_____

_____

_____

_____

_____

_____

_____

_____

_____

_____

_____

_____

_____

_____

_____

_____

_____

_____

_____

_____

_____

Chapter 34: The Power of Perception in Public Speaking - Cultivating Awareness to Enhance Understanding and Connection

Engaging in a Perceptive Discussion

As we gather once more in our shared exploration of public speaking, let's delve into the power of perception. Imagine us engaged in a thoughtful conversation about how awareness of perception—both your own and your audience's—can profoundly enhance your connection and understanding.

Understanding Your Own Perception

Perception in speaking begins with self-awareness. It's about understanding how your views, biases, and experiences shape the way you communicate. Reflect on a past speaking experience. How did your perception influence the way you delivered your message?

Tuning into Your Audience's Perception
Just as crucial understands your audience's perception. This involves considering their backgrounds, beliefs, and current state of mind. How do you assess your audience's perceptions before and during your speech, and how does this influence your approach?

Interplay of Speaker and Audience Perceptions
Effective public speaking is often a dance between the speaker's and the audience's perceptions. It's about finding common ground, challenging assumptions, and opening new perspectives. How do you navigate this interplay in your talks?

Overcoming Perceptual Barriers

Perceptual barriers can hinder communication. These might include preconceived notions, cultural differences, or misunderstandings. What strategies do you employ to identify and overcome these barriers in your public speaking?

Practical Exercise: The Perception Check

This practical exercise, The Perception Check, takes a recent communication and analyses it from the perspective of the listener. Consider how various backgrounds or beliefs might interpret your message. Reflect on how this exercise might alter your approach to future talks for more effective communication.

Reflecting On the Truth

As we wrap up this chapter, think about the role perception plays in public speaking. Awareness of both your own and your audience's perceptions is key to delivering messages that resonate and connect. It's not just about what you say, but how it's heard and understood. Cultivating this awareness can transform good speeches into truly impactful and meaningful engagements.

NOTES

_____

_____

_____

_____

_____

_____

_____

_____

_____

_____

_____

_____

_____

_____

_____

_____

_____

_____

_____

Chapter 35: Mental Dynamics in Oratory - Influences and Formations - Exploring the Psychological Aspects of Speech Preparation and Delivery

Delving into a Deep Psychological Exploration

Let's gather again in our ongoing journey through the art of public speaking, turning our attention to the mental dynamics that underpin oratory. Picture this as a conversation that delves deep into the psychological facets of preparing and delivering speeches.

The Speaker's Mindflow: A Key Influencer

The mindflow you bring to your speaking engagements profoundly impacts your performance. It encompasses your thoughts, attitudes, and mental states during both preparation and delivery. Reflect on a speaking experience: How did your mindflow at that time shape your performance, for better or worse?

Navigating Mental Formations

Our beliefs, experiences, and biases, the mental formations we carry, critically influence our approach to public speaking. These mental constructs can either empower or constrain us. How do you engage with these internal formations to enhance your effectiveness as a speaker?

Tackling Nervousness and Anxiety

Nervousness and anxiety are natural companions to public speaking. Effectively managing these feelings is essential for a confident and impactful delivery. What strategies do you employ to keep these emotions in check and maintain poise during your communication?

Harnessing the Power of Visualisation

Positive visualisation can be a transformative technique in speech preparation. It involves envisioning yourself delivering your speech successfully, engaging with your audience, and navigating challenges with ease. How frequently do you incorporate visualisation into your preparation, and how does it influence your delivery?

Psychological Resilience in Speaking

Building psychological resilience is key to enduring the ups and downs of public speaking. It's about developing a mental toughness that allows you to handle criticism, learn from mistakes, and come back stronger. What practices do you follow to build resilience in your communication?

Practical Exercise: Mental Rehearsal

As a practical exercise the Mental Rehearsal, before your next speaking engagement, take some time to mentally rehearse your presentation. Visualize the setting, your delivery, the audience's reactions, and even how you handle potential mishaps. Reflect on this mental rehearsal afterward: Did it help in aligning your actual performance with your envisioned one?

Reflecting On the Truth

In closing this chapter, consider the profound impact of mental dynamics in oratory. The psychological aspects of preparing and delivering a speech are as crucial as the content itself. Mastering these mental dynamics can elevate your public speaking, transforming it from a mere skill to a profound and impactful art form.

NOTES

_____

_____

_____

_____

_____

_____

_____

_____

_____

_____

_____

_____

_____

_____

_____

_____

_____

_____

_____

_____

Chapter 36: Conscious Communication - Elevating Awareness - Developing Deep Consciousness for Profound Speaking Experiences

Immersing Ourselves in a Deep Conversation

Let us reconvene in our enlightening exploration of public speaking, this time turning our focus to the concept of conscious communication. Picture us engaged in a lively, thoughtful discussion, exploring how deepening your consciousness can lead to more profound and impactful speaking experiences.

The Essence of Consciousness in Speaking

Conscious communication is about more than the words you choose; it's about a heightened awareness of your message, your audience, and the context of your speech. It involves being fully present and deeply connected to every aspect of your speaking engagement. Reflect on a time when you were truly 'in the moment' while speaking. What impact did that have on your delivery and your audience's reception?

Developing a Deeper Awareness

Deepening your awareness as a speaker involves tuning into both the seen and unseen elements of your communication. It's about understanding the subtleties of body language, tone, and emotion, both in yourself and your audience. How do you cultivate this deeper sense of awareness in your preparations and presentations?

The Impact of Mindful Speaking

Mindful speaking transforms standard speeches into memorable, impactful experiences. It allows you to connect with your audience on a deeper level, making your message more resonant and relatable. How has mindfulness influenced your effectiveness as a speaker?

Nurturing Empathy and Connection

Conscious communication is deeply rooted in empathy. It's about truly understanding and connecting with your audience's needs, emotions, and expectations. What strategies do you use to foster empathy and connection in your speaking engagements?

Practical Exercise: The Consciousness Drill

The practical exercise called The Consciousness Drill, during your next speech preparation; take a moment to fully engage with the material. Consider not just the content but the deeper implications of your message. While delivering, focus on being fully present and connected with your audience. Afterward, reflect on how this conscious approach influenced the interaction.

Reflecting On the Truth

As we conclude this chapter, ponder the transformative power of conscious communication. It's about more than just delivering a well-crafted speech; it's about creating an experience that resonates on a deeper level, both for you and your audience. This deeper level of consciousness in your communication can lead to more meaningful and profound speaking experiences.

NOTES

Chapter 37: The Illusion of the Fixed Speaker - Embracing Flexibility and Adaptability in Your Speaking Identity

Delving into a Dynamic Discussion

As we come together once more in our exploration of public speaking, let's challenge the notion of a fixed speaking identity. Imagine us engaging in a fluid conversation, examining the benefits of embracing flexibility and adaptability in how you present yourself as a speaker.

Challenging Fixed Speaking Style

The idea of a fixed speaking style is an illusion. As speakers, we often pigeonhole ourselves into a certain style or persona, but true effectiveness in speaking comes from being adaptable. Think about a time when adapting your speaking style had a positive impact. What did that experience teach you about flexibility in speaking?

The Benefits of an Adaptable Approach

Being adaptable in public speaking allows you to connect with a wider range of audiences and situations. It means tailoring your message, tone, and style to fit the context and audience's needs. How do you assess and adapt to different speaking scenarios?

Overcoming the Fear of Change

One barrier to embracing adaptability is the fear of losing one's 'signature style' or comfort zone. However, growth as a speaker requires stepping out of these confines. How have you confronted and overcome this fear in your speaking journey?

The Role of Continuous Learning

Adaptability in speaking is fueled by continuous learning. It involves staying open to new ideas, techniques, and feedback. What strategies do you employ to continuously evolve and expand your speaking capabilities?

Practical Exercise: The Adaptability Challenge

This practical exercise called The Adaptability Challenge, prepare a short speech and then practice delivering it in different styles: formal, casual, storytelling, or instructional. Notice how changing your style affects your delivery and message. Reflect on the flexibility this brings to your speaking and how it could be applied to various speaking engagements.

Reflecting On the Truth

In concluding this chapter, think about the illusion of a fixed speaker identity and the power of embracing flexibility. An adaptable speaker is not confined to a single identity but is versatile, responsive, and continually evolving. This approach enriches your speaking experiences and deepens your connection with diverse audiences.

NOTES

_____

_____

_____

_____

_____

_____

_____

_____

_____

_____

_____

_____

_____

_____

_____

_____

_____

_____

_____

_____

_____

_____

_____

_____

Chapter 38: The Speaker and the Environment - An Inseparable Bond - Exploring the Interconnectedness of the Speaker with the Audience and Setting

Engaging in an Interactive Dialogue

As we come together again in our exploration of public speaking, let's turn our attention to the intricate relationship between the speaker, the audience, and the environment. Think of this as a dynamic conversation about how these elements are interconnected and how they influence your effectiveness as a speaker.

The Speaker-Audience Relationship

The connection between a speaker and their audience is fundamental. It's a two-way interaction where each influences and responds to the other. Reflect on a time when your interaction with the audience significantly changed the course or impact of your speech. What did this experience teach you about the speaker-audience relationship?

Adapting to Different Environments

Every speaking environment has its unique characteristics, whether it's a large auditorium, a small meeting room, or a virtual setting. How you adapt to these environments can greatly affect your delivery and connection with the audience. How do you prepare for and adjust to different speaking environments?

Sensitivity to Contextual Dynamics

Being sensitive to the contextual dynamics - the mood, the cultural setting, and the occasion - is crucial. It involves tuning into subtle cues and adjusting your tone, content, and delivery accordingly. How do you read and respond to these contextual dynamics in your speeches?

Creating an Engaging Atmosphere

Part of your role as a speaker is to create an atmosphere that engages your audience. This might involve using storytelling, humor, or rhetorical questions to draw your audience into your narrative. What techniques do you use to create an engaging atmosphere, regardless of the setting?

Practical Exercise: Environmental Adaptation

For a practical exercise called Environmental Adaptation, recall a recent speech or presentation. Reflect on how you adapted (or could have adapted) to the specific environment and audience dynamics. Consider the changes you made (or could make) in your approach, style, or content to better suit the setting and audience.

Reflecting On the Truth

In concluding this chapter, think about the inseparable bond between you as the speaker, your audience, and the environment. Recognising and harnessing this interconnectedness is key to enhancing your effectiveness and impact as a speaker. It's about creating a harmonious dialogue where you, the audience, and the setting are in sync, each contributing to a memorable and impactful speaking experience.

NOTES

_____

_____

_____

_____

_____

_____

_____

_____

_____

_____

_____

_____

_____

_____

_____

_____

_____

_____

_____

_____

_____

_____

_____

_____

_____

_____

_____

_____

_____

_____

_____

_____

_____

_____

_____

_____

_____

_____

_____

_____

_____

Chapter 39: The Impermanence of Speaking - Navigating the Ever-Changing Landscape of Public Communication

Engaging in a Thoughtful Exchange

As we gather once more on our public speaking journey, let's discuss the concept of impermanence in the context of communication. Picture this as a vibrant conversation about navigating and embracing the constantly evolving landscape of public speaking.

Embracing Change in Public Speaking

The field of public speaking is ever-changing, with new technologies, shifting audience preferences, and evolving communication channels. Reflect on how changes in the public speaking landscape have impacted your approach. How have you adapted to these shifts over time?

The Transience of Speaking Styles

Speaking styles and trends come and go. What resonates with an audience today may not have the same impact tomorrow. Consider how your speaking style has evolved. What influenced these changes, and how have they affected your effectiveness as a speaker?

Keeping Up with Technological Advancements

Technology plays a significant role in the impermanence of public speaking. From virtual platforms to interactive tools, technology continuously reshapes the way we communicate. How do you stay abreast of these technological changes, and how have you integrated them into your speaking engagements?

Adapting to Audience Dynamics

Audience dynamics are also in a state of flux. Demographics, attention spans, and cultural contexts are shifting. How do you tune into and adapt to the changing needs and characteristics of your audience?

The Lifelong Learning of a Speaker

In a field marked by impermanence, lifelong learning becomes crucial. It's about continually updating your skills, seeking new knowledge, and being open to feedback. What are your strategies for ongoing learning and development in public speaking?

Practical Exercise: The Adaptation Review

The practical exercise called The Adaptation Review; think about your most recent speaking engagement. How did you adapt to the specific requirements of this event in terms of style, technology, or audience engagement? Reflect on what worked well and what could be improved in terms of adapting to the ever-changing landscape of public communication.

Reflecting On the Truth

As we conclude this chapter, consider the significance of impermanence in public speaking. Embracing this constant state of change is not just about staying relevant; it's about continually finding new ways to connect with your audience, share your message, and make a lasting impact. The ever-changing nature of public communication is not a challenge to overcome but an opportunity to continually grow and evolve as a speaker.

NOTES

Chapter 40: Attachment and Letting Go in Public Speaking - Finding Freedom in Embracing Change and Releasing Expectations

Delving into a Candid Conversation

Let's come together again in our exploration of public speaking, this time to discuss the concepts of attachment and letting go. Imagine this as an open, honest conversation about how releasing certain expectations can liberate and transform your approach to speaking.

Understanding Attachment in Speaking

In public speaking, attachment often manifests as clinging to certain outcomes, styles, or perceptions of success. Reflect on your speaking experiences. Have you ever been attached to a specific outcome or reaction from your audience? How did this attachment affect your performance and mindflow?

The Freedom of Letting Go

Letting go in public speaking means releasing rigid expectations and being open to various outcomes. It's about flexibility and adaptability, allowing you to respond more freely and authentically in the moment. How do you practice letting go of expectations during your speaking engagements?

Embracing change and uncertainty

Part of letting go is embracing the inherent change and uncertainty of public speaking. It means being prepared yet open to the unexpected, whether it's audience reactions, technical issues, or your own performance. How do you manage and embrace the unpredictable nature of speaking?

Balance between Preparation and Spontaneity

While preparation is key, overly rigid planning can lead to attachment to specific scripts or outcomes. Balancing preparation with the ability to be spontaneous allows for more genuine and engaging presentations. What strategies do you use to strike this balance?

Practical Exercise: Letting Go

For a practical exercise, Letting Go, choose an upcoming speaking engagement and consciously decide to release a specific expectation you have about it. This could be related to audience reaction, your delivery, or the impact of your speech. After the event, reflect on how letting go of this expectation affected your experience and performance.

Reflecting On the Truth

In concluding this chapter, think about the power of attachment and the freedom found in letting go. Releasing rigid expectations in public speaking opens a space for more authentic, adaptive, and responsive communication. It's about finding a sense of freedom and presence that allows you to connect more deeply with your audience and deliver your message in the most impactful way.

NOTES

_____

_____

_____

_____

_____

_____

_____

_____

_____

_____

_____

_____

_____

_____

_____

_____

_____

_____

_____

_____

Chapter 41: The Art of the Sitting Speaker - Embodying Stability and Mindfulness in Seated Communication

Engaging in an Intimate Discussion

As we gather again in our exploration of public speaking, let's focus on a less discussed yet important aspect: the art of sitting while speaking. Imagine this as a conversation about how being seated can influence and enhance your communication.

The Significance of Seated Speaking

Speaking while seated presents unique opportunities and challenges. It's a posture often associated with interviews, panel discussions, or virtual meetings. Reflect on your experiences speaking while seated. How does it differ from standing, and what adjustments do you find necessary?

Embodying Stability in a Seated Position
Stability in a seated position is about more than physical balance; it's about conveying a sense of groundedness and confidence. It involves mindful posture, deliberate gestures, and the effective use of your upper body to communicate. How do you ensure your seated posture contributes positively to your message?

Mindfulness and Presence
Being seated can enhance mindfulness and presence. It allows you to be more grounded and potentially more focused. Consider how being seated affects your ability to be present both with your material and with your audience. How does this change the way you engage with your content and listeners?

Communicating Effectively from a Seat

Effective seated communication requires mindful use of voice, facial expressions, and upper body movements. It's about maximising the impact of your words through deliberate and expressive upper-body language. What techniques do you use to ensure your message is conveyed effectively when seated?

Practical Exercise: Seated Speaking Practice

For a practical exercise called Seated Speaking Practice," prepare a short speech or presentation to deliver while seated. Focus on your posture, gestures, and facial expressions. Record yourself, if possible, and afterward, watch the recording to observe how your seated posture influenced your delivery. Reflect on areas for improvement and strengths in your seated speaking style.

Reflecting On the Truth

In concluding this chapter, consider the unique dynamics of seated communication. The art of the sitting speaker is about harnessing stability, mindfulness, and expressiveness, even within the physical constraints of sitting. It's about understanding and utilising the nuances of this position to enhance your communication effectiveness.

NOTES

_____

_____

_____

_____

_____

_____

_____

_____

_____

_____

_____

_____

_____

_____

_____

_____

_____

_____

_____

_____

_____

_____

_____

_____

_____

_____

_____

_____

_____

_____

_____

_____

_____

_____

_____

_____

_____

_____

_____

_____

_____

Chapter 42: The Dynamics of Standing Oratory Harnessing Energy and Command in Upright Expression

Engaging in an Energetic Dialogue

As we reconvene in our continuous journey through the nuances of public speaking, let's shift our focus to the dynamics of standing oratory. Imagine this as a lively discussion about the energy and command inherent in upright expression and how they can be harnessed to elevate your speaking.

The Power of Standing in Public Speaking

Standing while speaking brings a different energy compared to sitting. It allows for a more commanding presence and the opportunity to physically engage with your space. Reflect on your experiences of speaking while standing. How do your energy and audience engagement change in this position?

Utilising Physical Space

When standing, you have the advantage of using physical space more dynamically. This includes moving across the stage or room, using purposeful gestures, and managing proximity to the audience. How do you use physical space to enhance your message and engage with your audience?

Harnessing Posture and Movement

Effective standing oratory involves more than just standing up; it's about how you hold yourself and move. A confident posture and deliberate movements can significantly impact your speech's effectiveness. What are your strategies for maintaining a strong posture and using movement effectively?

The Impact of Upright Energy

Standing up naturally injects a different kind of energy into your delivery, both in your voice and your physicality. This energy can be harnessed to drive home points, engage the audience, and create a memorable experience. How do you manage and channel this energy in your speeches?

Practical Exercise: The Movement Mapping Drill

The practical exercise called the Movement Mapping Drill; plan a short speech where you consciously incorporate movement. Map out where you will move during different parts of your speech, how you will use gestures, and where you will direct your focus. After delivering this speech, reflect on how these elements influenced your delivery and the audience's response.

Reflecting On the Truth

As we wrap up this chapter, think about the dynamic nature of standing oratory. Standing to speak is not merely a physical act; it's an opportunity to harness energy, command attention, and physically embody your message. It's about using your entire being to communicate effectively, making your speech not alone be heard but felt and remembered.

NOTES

_____

_____

_____

_____

_____

_____

_____

_____

_____

_____

_____

_____

_____

_____

_____

_____

_____

_____

_____

Chapter 43: The Grace of the Reclining Communicator - Conveying Ease and Reflection in Relaxed Postures

Engaging Relaxed with Reflective Conversation

As we gather once more on our public speaking journey, let's explore a less conventional but equally important aspect: the grace of the reclining communicator. Envision this discussion as an exploration of how relaxed postures can convey ease, thoughtfulness, and reflection in communication.

Unconventional Power of Reclining Postures

Reclining or relaxed postures in communication often signal ease and approachability. They can create a more intimate and reflective atmosphere, breaking down barriers between speaker and audience. Reflect on experiences where a more relaxed posture impacted the tone and reception of your communication. How did it change the dynamic?

Balancing Relaxation with Engagement

While reclining postures are more relaxed, it's crucial to balance this with active engagement. This involves maintaining a presence that is open and inviting, ensuring your audience feels connected to you and your message. How do you achieve this balance when adopting a more relaxed posture?

Using Relaxed Postures to Enhance Storytelling

Relaxed postures can be particularly effective in storytelling or conversational settings. They can make narratives feel more personal and authentic. Think about how adopting a more casual posture could enhance the storytelling aspects of your communication.

The Subtleties of Non-Verbal Communication

In a reclined or relaxed posture, non-verbal communication becomes even more significant. It's about using facial expressions, eye contact, and subtle gestures to convey your message effectively. How do you ensure that your non-verbal cues remain strong and clear, even in a more relaxed stance?

Practical Exercise: Reclined Speech Practice

For a practical exercise called the Reclined Speech Practice, deliver part of a speech or a story in a relaxed, reclined posture. Focus on maintaining an engaging presence through your facial expressions, vocal tone, and eye contact. Afterward, reflect on how this posture affected your delivery style and audience engagement.

Reflecting On the Truth

In closing this chapter, consider the unique qualities that reclining communication brings to the table. While less conventional, it offers a chance to convey messages in a manner that is approachable, reflective, and intimately engaging. The grace of the reclining communicator lies in the ability to remain relaxed yet compelling, offering a different and powerful mode of connection with your audience.

NOTES

_____

_____

_____

_____

_____

_____

_____

_____

_____

_____

_____

_____

_____

_____

_____

_____

_____

_____

_____

Chapter 44: The Language of Gestures - Harnessing Non-Verbal Communication in Public Speaking

Engaging in a Meaningful Exploration

As we reach the final chapter of our exploration of public speaking, let's delve into the profound world of non-verbal communication. Imagine this as a deep dive into the language of gestures, where we explore how the unspoken elements of body language and mudras can significantly enhance your public speaking.

Power of Non-Verbal Communication

Non-verbal communication, or the language of gestures, plays a crucial role in public speaking. It encompasses everything from facial expressions and body movements to posture and hand gestures (akin to mudras in their communicative power). Reflect on an instance where a speaker's body language left a strong impression on you. What did it communicate beyond words?

The Subtlety and Strength of Gestures

Gestures can convey a range of emotions and messages, often more powerfully than words. They can emphasize a point, convey sincerity, or build a connection with the audience. Consider how you use gestures in your speaking. Are they intentional, and how do they align with the messages you're conveying?

Cultivating Awareness of Body Language

Being aware of your body language and consciously cultivating it can transform your speaking. This involves understanding how different gestures can be perceived and using them to reinforce your message. How do you ensure that your body language is consistent with your spoken words?

The Impact of Cultural Contexts on Gestures
It's important to consider the cultural context of gestures. What might be a positive gesture in one culture could be offensive in another. How do you navigate these cultural nuances in your speaking, especially when addressing diverse audiences?

Practical Exercise: The Gesture Alignment Drill
For a practical exercise called the Gesture Alignment Drill, record a speech or presentation focusing on your use of gestures. Watch it again, paying close attention to your body language. Reflect on whether your gestures align with and enhance your message. Consider how different gestures might be perceived and how they could be refined for clarity and impact.

Reflecting On the Truth

As we conclude, think about the silent yet impactful language of gestures in public speaking. Just like mudras in Buddhism, each gesture you make holds the potential to communicate volumes, often reaching the audience on a deeper, more intuitive level. Mastering this language is about harmonizing your non-verbal cues with your verbal communication, creating a seamless and powerful speaking experience.

NOTES

_____

_____

_____

_____

_____

_____

_____

_____

_____

_____

_____

_____

_____

_____

_____

_____

_____

_____

Closing Thoughts: The Journey towards Mindful Communication

Dear Reader,

As we close the pages of this book, it's essential to reflect on the journey we've embarked upon together. Through each chapter, we've explored the multifaceted art of public speaking, beyond been a skill but as a profound means of connection and transformation.

Summary of Key Learnings:

The Power of Presence: Being fully present in every speaking engagement invites a deeper connection with your audience. Your undivided attention makes them feel valued and heard, creating a space for meaningful interaction.

This presence is the foundation upon which trust and rapport are built.

Embracing Change: The willingness to adapt and evolve is crucial in the ever-changing landscape of public communication. As audiences and contexts shift, so must your approach to engagement and message delivery. Embrace change as an opportunity to grow and innovate in your speaking endeavors.

Cultivating Mindfulness: Mindful communication goes beyond words, encompassing empathy, understanding, and genuine connection. It involves active listening, being fully in the moment, and responding to the underlying emotions of the audience. This approach deepens the impact of the message and fosters a truly collaborative dialogue.

Harnessing Verbal, Visual, and Vocal Cues: Utilize the power of gestures, expressions, voice tone, and word choice to enhance your message. These elements together convey emotion and intent, adding depth to the spoken words. Effective use of these cues can transform a simple message into a memorable experience.

Building and Developing Authentic Relationships: Foster genuine connections with your audience through sincere and authentic communication. Show your true self, sharing your values and vulnerabilities, to create a bond that extends beyond the speaking platform. Authentic relationships are the cornerstone of impactful public speaking.

Adaptability and Engagement: Adjust your speaking style for different audiences and encourage interactive participation for a dynamic and inclusive environment. Being adaptable shows respect for your audience's unique needs and preferences. Engagement transforms passive listening into a shared, active experience.

Embracing Mindflow for Antifragility: Develop 'mindflow' to not only withstand challenges but also to grow stronger from them. This state of flow aligns your skills and tasks with the challenges at hand, making you resilient and antifragile. As you embrace mindflow, you turn adversity into a catalyst for growth.

Continuous Learning: Public speaking is a journey, not a destination. There's always more to learn, more to refine, and more to discover. Treat every speaking opportunity as a learning experience and remain open to feedback and new ideas to master the art of communication.

Encouragement for Continuous Practice and Improvement: Your journey as a speaker does not end here. With every talk, every presentation, and every conversation, you have the opportunity to practice and improve. The path to becoming a mindful communicator is ongoing—a path that you shape with every word you utter and every silence you honor.

Embrace this journey with the understanding that every effort you make contributes to a larger purpose—a world where communication is not effective but empathetic, not only clear but compassionate.

The Dream: A Billion Minds Inspired

Remember the vision that has guided these chapters: to inspire 1 billion people to embrace the art of public speaking and to communicate with intention and mindfulness. This dream is a call to action, urging you to use your voice for the greater good and to be a beacon of positive change in how we interact and understand one another.

Your Role in This Movement

You are an integral part of this transformative movement. Every time you choose to communicate mindfully, you contribute to a global shift towards more meaningful and heartfelt interactions. Your commitment to practicing the principles outlined in this book is a step towards a world that values understanding and kindness.

Together, we can

Join me in this mission. Let each speaking opportunity be a step towards empowering not just yourself but those around you. Share your journey, encourage others to find their voice, and together, let's cultivate a culture of mindful communication.

As we part ways in this book, let the conversations continue beyond the written word. Take these lessons, apply them in your life, and become an ambassador for a way of speaking—and living—that cherishes every moment as an opportunity to connect, to grow, and to unite.

Let's begin

We will start this journey not as individuals but as a collective—moving towards a world more connected, more understanding, and profoundly more compassionate.

With trust and determination,

Rohit Bassi
www.rohitbassi.com

REFERENCE

1. "The Miracle of Mindfulness" by Thich Nhat Hanh

2. "Talk Like TED" by Carmine Gallo

3. "Peace Is Every Step" by Thich Nhat Hanh

4. "The Art of Public Speaking" by Stephen E. Lucas

5. "The Art of Communicating" by Thich Nhat Hanh

6. "How to Win Friends and Influence People" by Dale Carnegie

7. "Fear: Essential Wisdom for Getting Through the Storm" by Thich Nhat Hanh

8. "Mindful Communication in the Age of Distraction" by Elizabeth Morrison

9. "Zen Mind, Beginner's Mind" by Shunryu Suzuki

10. "The Power of Now" by Eckhart Tolle

11. "The Art of Happiness" by Dalai Lama

12. "Thinking, Fast and Slow" by Daniel Kahneman

13. "The Tao of Communication: A Study in the Philosophy of Communication" by J. J. Clarke

14. "The Ethics of Rhetoric" by Richard M. Weaver

15. "The Way of the Heart" by Henri Nouwen

16. "Daring Greatly" by Brené Brown

17. "Autobiography of a Yogi" by Paramahansa Yogananda

18. "Emotional Intelligence" by Daniel Goleman

19. "The Book of Secrets" by Osho

20. "Nonviolent Communication" by Marshall B. Rosenberg

21. "Be Here Now" by Ram Dass

22. "The Culture Map" by Erin Meyer

23. "The Heart of the Buddha's Teaching" by Thich Nhat Hanh

24. "Kiss, Bow, or Shake Hands" by Terri Morrison and Wayne A. Conaway

25. "The Dhammapada" (various translations available)

26. "Crucial Conversations" by Kerry Patterson et al.

27. "The Bhagavad Gita" (various translations and commentaries available)

28. "The Charisma Myth" by Olivia Fox Cabane

29. "I Ching: The Book of Changes" (various translations available)

30. "Influence" by Robert B. Cialdini

31. "Tao Te Ching" by Lao Tzu (various translations available)

32. "Quiet" by Susan Cain

33. "The Upanishads" (various translations and commentaries available)

34. "Made to Stick" by Chip Heath and Dan Heath

35. "The Essential Rumi" by Jalaluddin Rumi (translated by Coleman Barks)

36. "Drive" by Daniel H. Pink

37. "The Yoga Sutras of Patanjali" (various translations and commentaries available)

38. "Start with Why" by Simon Sinek

39. "Awakening the Buddha Within" by Lama Surya Das

40. "The Five Dysfunctions of a Team" by Patrick Lencioni

41. "The Tibetan Book of Living and Dying" by Sogyal Rinpoche

42. "Good to Great" by Jim Collins

43. "The Way of Zen" by Alan Watts

44. "The Seven Habits of Highly Effective People" by Stephen R. Covey

45. "Siddhartha" by Hermann Hesse

46. "When Awareness Becomes Natural: A Guide to Cultivating Mindfulness in Everyday Life" by Sayadaw U Tejaniya

47. "The Art of Living: Peace and Freedom in the Here and Now" by Thich Nhat Hanh

48. "Who Ordered This Truckload of Dung?: Inspiring Stories for Welcoming Life's Difficulties" by Ajahn Brahm

49. "The Sound of Silence: The Selected Teachings of Ajahn Sumedho" by Ajahn Sumedho

    "Being Peace" by Thich Nhat Hanh

50. "Food for the Heart: The Collected Teachings of Ajahn Chah" by Ajahn Chah

51. "No Mud, No Lotus: The Art of Transforming Suffering" by Thich Nhat Hanh

52. "Old Path White Clouds: Walking in the Footsteps of the Buddha" by Thich Nhat Hanh

53. "The Heart of the Buddha's Teaching: Transforming Suffering into Peace, Joy, and Liberation" by Thich Nhat Hanh

54. "A Guide to the Bodhisattva's Way of Life" by Shantideva

55. "The Book of Five Rings" by Miyamoto Musashi

56. "The Art of War" by Sun Tzu

57. "Hagakure: The Book of the Samurai" by Yamamoto